Make Your Stand

Drew Kizer

Make Your Stand
Copyright © 2003 by Drew Kizer
          6909 Timber Trail Road
          Leeds, AL 35094

Published by Riddle Creek Publishing
          232 County Road 19
          Haleyville, AL 35565-7416
          http://www.riddlecreekpublishing.com

Cover design by April Miller and Allison Kizer

All scripture quotations, unless otherwise indicated, are taken from *The Holy Bible; English Standard Version.* Copyright © 2001 by Crossway Bibles.

ISBN 0-9725894-1-4

Make Your Stand

Table of Contents

Introduction
Stand for Something.................................. 1

The Essence of Standing 11

Objections... 21

The Offensive
Stand For Your Faith............................... 29

Stand For Yourself.................................. 39

Stand For The Truth 51

Stand For Worship.................................. 61

Stand For Modesty 73

The Defensive
Stand Against Satan 83

Stand Against God's Enemies................... 93

Stand Against Drinking 101

Stand Against Addiction 109

Stand Against Peer Pressure 119

Endnotes...127

1
Stand for Something

There's an old saying, "There's nothing in the middle of the road but a yellow line and dead possums." If that is the case, the number of yellow lines and dead possums is growing.

Moral stances and ideas based on things like "right" and "wrong" are unpopular these days. People are searching for "middle ground," and as a result few are really standing for anything. Our conversations are starting to sound like a scene from *Fiddler on the Roof*. In this movie, a middle-aged Jewish father named Tevya is making milk deliveries to one of the villages on his route. He is talking with a young rebel named Parchek and an older man named Mordecai, who is comfortable with the Jewish traditions. The three of them are confused about the times in which they live, and they are trying to make sense of it all. Parchek says, "You cannot close your eyes to what's happening in the world today." Tevya says, "You're right." Then Mordecai says, "Ah! But tradition. We must stay in the old ways." Tevya says, "You're right." Parchek then says, "We cannot both be right." And Tevya says, "You know, you're right, too." Many of us can sympathize with poor Tevya. In the face of so many changes, we want to throw up our hands and conclude that everyone is right![1]

We live in the postmodern age, an age characterized by tolerance and a refusal to admit anything is truly right or wrong. Today truth is a matter of one's opinion. That may be humorous when watching *Fiddler on the*

Roof, but in real-life application, it is frightening. For example, an article in *U.S. News and World Report* recently reported that ten to twenty percent of the students in many college classes would not say that the extermination of millions of Jews during Hitler's regime was morally wrong, even though they personally found it despicable.[2] The situation is degenerating to the point where we are debating whether or not the cold-blooded murder of millions of innocent people was wrong! What is this world coming to?

We must stand for something. In other words, Christians need to declare themselves. We cannot stay in hiding. Instead, we must openly profess our beliefs and true identity to the world around us. A disciple cannot possibly be a part of the church, the "pillar and buttress of truth" (1 Timothy 3:15), without standing *for* Christ and *against* evil. Christianity loses all meaning when we fail to stand.

I Must Stand For Something

Standing for something is logical. It doesn't make sense to say, "I am not taking a stand because nothing is absolutely true. Nothing is real—you have your truth and I have mine. Let's just tolerate one another and live at peace." When a person says, "I am not taking a stand," he has already contradicted himself. He is standing for not taking a stand!

Those who oppose standing for something usually cite tolerance as the reason for their attitude. They promote themselves as friendly and agreeable. They would have us believe they are absolutely comfortable with all opinions and beliefs, but their message is deceptive. The word "tolerance" implies disagreement. A person doesn't "tolerate" someone with whom he agrees. Jesus was right. No one can serve two masters (Matthew 6:24). In reality, "straddling the fence" is impossible.

Standing for something is not only logically necessary, but it is also scripturally necessary. This is the case from Genesis to Revelation. Consider the following examples:

1. As Moses prepared the children of Israel to enter Canaan and conquer it, he gave them two choices. There was no room for middle ground. Deuteronomy 30:19-20 reads,

> I call heaven and earth to witness against you today, that I have set before you life and death, blessing and curse. Therefore choose life, that you and your offspring may live, loving the Lord your God, obeying his voice and holding fast to him....

2. Observe that Joshua commanded the Israelites, "...choose this day whom you will serve...But as for me and my house, we will serve the Lord" (Joshua 24:15).

3. Elijah asked his indecisive nation, "How long will you go limping between two different opinions?" (1 Kings 18:21).

4. Jesus stated in His Sermon on the Mount, "No one can serve two masters, for either he will hate the one and love the other, or he will be devoted to the one and despise the other..." (Matthew 6:24). Also, He shared this parable with a reluctant disciple: "No one who puts his hand to the plow and looks back is fit for the kingdom of God" (Luke 9:62).

5. Paul charged his readers to "Be watchful, stand firm in the faith, act like men, be strong" (1 Corinthians 16:13). Earlier, he had commanded them to "be steadfast, immovable, always abounding in the work of the Lord, knowing that in the Lord your labor is not in vain" (1 Corinthians 15:58).

6. After His ascension, Jesus sent these words by

John to the church at Laodicea: "I know your works: you are neither cold nor hot. Would that you were either cold or hot! So, because you are lukewarm, and neither hot nor cold, I will spit you out of my mouth" (Revelation 3:15-16).

I must stand for something. From a logical point of view, I am forced to. From a scriptural point of view, I am commanded to. We have a natural tendency to shy away from this. After all, standing *for* one thing means standing *against* something else. Christ never said following Him would be the easiest life, but He did say it would be the most rewarding life (Matthew 7:13-14).

I Must Stand for the Right Thing

It is not unusual to find people making a stand for something. But are they standing for the *right* thing? What about you? Are you standing for the right thing? Consider what the Bible teaches...

1. *I must stand "in the Lord"* (Philippians 4:1; 1 Thessalonians 3:8). This means I must "stand up for Jesus," confessing my faith in God's power to save. Often we casually discuss "confession" as a step of salvation, forgetting the price of confession during the first century. In those days, you could get your head chopped off for saying, "I believe that Jesus Christ is the Son of God." These are safer times, but confession should still be made boldly and publicly.

2. *I must stand "in the faith"* (1 Corinthians 16:13). The word "faith" can mean a number of things. Frequently it is used to designate our personal belief (Romans 5:1; Hebrews 11:1). But when Paul said, "Stand firm in the faith," he was using "faith" in the sense of the gospel (cf. 1 Corinthians 15:1).

In light of this, how should the Christian react when it becomes difficult to preach subjects like...

- The essentiality of baptism to salvation (Mark 16:16; Acts 2:38; 22:16; Romans 6:3-4; 1 Peter 3:21)?
- The sin of dividing the church into denominations (Ephesians 4:4)?
- The silence of the Scriptures on instrumental music in worship (Ephesians 5:19; Colossians 3:16)?
- Profane words and dirty jokes (Matthew 12:36-37; Ephesians 5:4)?
- Modest apparel (1 Timothy 2:9-10)?
- The inevitability of Judgment Day and the two eternal destinies: heaven and hell (2 Corinthians 5:10; Matthew 25:46)?

Even when it is difficult, the Christian must stand for the faith!

3. *I must stand for the freedom for which Christ has set us free* (Galatians 5:1). When it comes to taking a stand, we tend to concentrate only upon the laws and limitations God has placed upon us. But standing for what is right also includes standing for the freedoms Christ has given us.

Paul's purpose for writing his letter to the Galatians was principally to encourage his readers to leave the bondage of Judaism for the freedom of Christianity. Thus, we read, "For freedom Christ has set us free; stand firm therefore, and do not submit again to a yoke of slavery" (Galatians 5:1). Some Jewish Christians were trying to place a "yoke of slavery" upon the necks of their Gentile brethren. One of the major contentions was circumcision, which was ordered by the law of Moses (cf. Acts 15:5, 10). But Paul demonstrated that the law was a system of bondage, or slavery, and that in Christ we are freed from that bondage and adopted as sons (Galatians 4:5-7). He stood firm for casting off the yoke of the law of Moses and the traditions of men so that he might live according to the liberty found in Christ.

We also ought to stand for casting off the traditions

of men for simple New Testament Christianity. As the old preachers used to say, "In matters of faith, unity; in matters of opinion, liberty; in all things, charity."

4. *I must stand "in one spirit" with my brothers and sisters in Christ.* When Paul wrote to the Philippians he uttered the following prayer: "Only let your manner of life be worthy of the gospel of Christ, so that whether I come and see you or am absent, I may hear of you that you are standing firm in one spirit, with one mind striving side by side for the faith of the gospel" (Philippians 1:27). Like Jesus, he prayed for unity (John 17:20-23). If we want to do our part in answering these prayers, we must stand in one spirit, being joined together by a shared love for God's word. This is true unity: the "unity of the Spirit" (Ephesians 4:3-6).

God calls on us to stand for the right thing: for His Son, for the faith, for our freedom in Christ, and for the unity of the Spirit.

I Must Stand for the Right Thing, Or Else I Will Be Left With Nothing

Why do people tolerate so many things? Generally speaking, do we not try to be flexible or tolerant in an effort to gain something? A business executive may tolerate dishonesty in order to gain money. A politician may tolerate corruption so that he can gain votes. A teenager may tolerate foul language in order to gain friends. Tolerance is one of the most frequently used tools to gain things we need or want. But before we decide to seek out our desires through tolerance, we need to ask, "Who are we tolerating? Can they really give us what we need?"

Consider what James writes in James 1:6-8:

But let him ask [for wisdom] in faith, with no doubting, for the one who doubts is like a wave of the sea that is driven and tossed by the wind. For that person must not suppose that he will receive anything from the Lord; he is a double-minded man, unstable in all his ways.

Hear what he says about the one who doubts: "That person must not suppose that he will receive *anything* from the Lord." God gives us every good and perfect gift (James 1:17), but He will offer nothing but punishment to the one who doubts. When one refuses to take a stand, he has a problem with doubt. Doubt and Tolerance are close friends, and those who associate with them can expect to receive nothing but condemnation from the Father.

The Parable of the Talents in Matthew 25:14-30 is a perfect illustration of what those who refuse to take a stand will receive. A man with three servants decided to go on a journey. He entrusted these three men with some of his property, each according to his ability: to one he gave five talents, to another two, to another he gave one. When the master returned he called his servants together to settle accounts. The one who was entrusted with five talents had been working diligently. He had profited five talents more. His master commended him, saying, "Well done, good and faithful servant. You have been faithful over a little; I will set you over much. Enter into the joy of your master." The servant who was given two talents had also doubled his money and was given a similar commendation. However, the third servant who was given only one talent was afraid. He had neither toiled nor striven to produce anything. He opted rather for inaction and hid his talent in the ground. Upon hearing this, his master reacted angrily, saying, "You wicked and slothful servant!" Then he had that spineless, one-talent man cast into outer darkness, where there was "weeping and gnashing of teeth."

I must stand for the right thing, or else I will be left

with nothing but condemnation. God is calling for us to take a stand. Are we answering that call?

In actuality, all of us are standing for something whether we mean to or not. Some may be standing for the cause of the devil. Others may stand for their own preferences and desires. Others may stand only for fear, being guided by doubt and tolerance instead of a conviction of the truth. Hopefully you are standing for Jesus Christ, who always stands for you. He is our advocate in heaven, the One who died for us (1 John 2:1-2), and He wants everyone to stand with Him on the side of righteousness!

Exercises

Fill In The Blank
1. A Christian must stand for _____ and against _____.
2. The word "tolerance" implies _____.
3. No one can serve two _____.
4. God set before the Israelites life and death, _____ and _____.
5. Joshua said, "Choose this day whom you will _____."
6. Elijah asked, "How long will you go _____ between two different _____?"
7. Jesus rebuked the Laodiceans for being _____.
8. The price of _____ was costly in the first century.
9. "Faith" in this lesson is used in the sense of the _____.
10. Jesus prayed for _____.
11. Doubt and _____ are close friends.

Discussion
1. The Christian must stand for the *right* things. What does this mean? Can you give some examples?
2. What are some controversial subjects that make it difficult to stand for the gospel?
3. What does it mean to stand for your Christian freedom? Do some people try to remove this freedom? How?

2
The Essence of Standing

A young Episcopalian preacher named Dudly Tyng was once watching some workmen operate a corn-shelling machine during a break from his study. When he thoughtlessly moved too close to the apparatus, a sleeve of his coat got caught in a moving cog, and his arm was literally torn from his shoulder. Doctors tried to save him, but it was hopeless. Someone overheard the last words he uttered to his father, who was sitting by his side: *"Tell them to stand up for Jesus."* Inspired by these final words, the man wrote the following poem:

> Stand up, stand up for Jesus,
> Ye soldiers of the cross;
> Lift high His royal banner,
> It must not suffer loss:
> From vict'ry unto vict'ry
> His army shall He lead,
> Till ev'ry foe is vanquished,
> And Christ is Lord indeed.

Of course, this poem became the favorite hymn entitled, "Stand Up For Jesus."[3]

We sing many songs about standing. Sometimes we will even physically stand while singing them. But what does it mean to "stand up for Jesus?" What is the essence of standing?

In the last lesson we discussed how "standing" signifies a public declaration or an open profession.

Christians must "take a stand" by indicating their faith in Christ to the world around them by their words and their conduct. Having made that clear, let's engage in a deeper discussion by asking, "What is the essence of taking a stand for Jesus?"

A Conviction of the Truth

If you are standing for something, for what do you stand? It is not enough to answer, "I am standing for Jesus." How can you be certain? This world is filled with false teachers.

Many people have been hurt because they did not investigate the facts to arrive at the truth. For example, in November of 1970, 900 people in Guyana, South America, drank a poisonous concoction at the instruction of a so-called religious leader named Jim Jones. Many people died because they did not consider that their leader could be deceiving them. Similarly, in 1993 another cult figure named David Koresh led 76 people to their deaths in Waco, Texas. In more recent news, a young girl named Elizabeth Smart was abducted by a man who called himself "Immanuel." While he promoted himself as an enlightened spiritual guide, he was nothing but a perverted fraud.

We have been warned of false teachers. Jesus told His disciples to beware of "false christs and false prophets" (Matthew 24:24). Also, Paul mentions such a thing as "false apostles" and says, "even Satan disguises himself as an angel of light" (2 Corinthians 11:13-14). Then John says, "...many false prophets have gone out into the world" (1 John 4:1).

Opposing all falsehood, the apostle Paul commands us to "stand firm in the faith" (1 Corinthians 16:13). We have already established that "*the* faith" is more than personal belief. "Faith," as it is expressed here, represents the embodiment of God's revealed word, which is found in the Bible. When Paul says, "Stand firm in the faith," he means, "Be convicted of the truth revealed to you by God."

Reverence

Throughout the ages, the posture of standing has been understood as a symbol of reverence or respect. As a bride walks down the aisle, the wedding guests traditionally rise from their seats. Americans commonly stand during the singing of the national anthem. In church settings, it is not unusual for worshippers to stand during the singing of a hymn or for prayer. All of these examples demonstrate how this posture expresses the idea of reverence.

A number of biblical examples also illustrate this point. After captivity, when the Jews were restored to Jerusalem, there was a marvelous occasion when Ezra read the book of the law from morning until midday. When he opened the book, all the people stood up, and they remained in this position for the duration of the reading (Nehemiah 8:1-8). Also, King Solomon stood out of respect during the dedication of the temple in Jerusalem (1 Kings 8:22). In another example, a woman named Hannah prayed fervently that she might receive a child from the Lord. After some time, her prayers were answered, and she bore a son named Samuel. When she returned to the temple to fulfill the vow she made to God, she remarked to Eli the priest, "Oh my lord! As you live, my lord, I am the woman who was *standing here* in your presence, praying to the Lord" (1 Samuel 1:26, emp. added). Everything about Hannah—from her silent but moving lips, to the way that she stood in Eli's presence—spoke of her deep respect and awe of Almighty God.

Without proper reverence or fear, a Christian cannot stand for God as he should. The Pharisees appeared to stand for the Lord, but in truth they did not. Everything on the surface said they were righteous: They fasted, prayed, gave alms, and wore phylacteries (cf. Deuteronomy 6:8; 11:18). They even went so far as to tithe the herbs from their gardens! (Matthew 23:23). Outwardly they seemed to stand for the Lord, however they lacked humility and reverence. Consider the Pharisee whom Jesus described in Luke 18:11-12:

> The Pharisee, standing by himself, prayed thus: "God, I thank you that I am not like other men, extortioners, unjust, adulterers, or even like this tax collector. I fast twice a week; I give tithes of all that I get."

Jesus' assessment, then, was that the worship of the Pharisees (their own version of "standing") was "vain" (Matthew 15:8-9).

On the other hand, the Old Testament is full of examples of faithful men and women who made a stand. And underlying every one of them is a proper attitude of fear and respect for the Creator.

- In Noah's day, "the wickedness of man was great in the earth, and...every intention of the thoughts of his heart was only evil continually" (Genesis 6:5). How did that patriarch stand alone in his wicked generation? According to the New Testament, he did so "in reverent fear" (Hebrews 11:7).

- During the Egyptian captivity of the Israelites, Pharaoh issued an edict to the Hebrew midwives saying they must kill all Hebrew baby boys. But they bravely defied the king. Why? They "feared God" (Exodus 1:17, 21).

- Obadiah was an official over the household of cruel King Ahab. Ahab's wife, Jezebel, was known as one of the fiercest enemies of the prophets of God this world has ever known; she could even scare Elijah!

But when Obadiah heard that she was murdering the prophets of the Lord, he secretly hid 100 of them in caves. Why? He "feared the Lord greatly" (1 Kings 18:3).

- Nehemiah, the great governor of Judea during the restoration period of Israel, broke precedent in refusing to wage heavy tax burdens upon God's people. Why? "Because of the fear of God" (Nehemiah 5:15).

So, a true stance for God is supported by an underpinning of fear. Those who wish to declare themselves do so in reverence and awe for Jehovah.

Commitment

Christians are called to be "steadfast, immovable, always abounding in the work of the Lord..." (1 Corinthians 15:58). The call to commitment and dedication is part of "standing up for Jesus."

Really, disciples are asked to do nothing more than what has already been done by God on their behalf. The Lord demonstrates perfect commitment and faithfulness in all of His activity (Isaiah 46:10; 1 Corinthians 1:9; 1 Thessalonians 5:24; 2 Thessalonians 3:3).

Unfortunately, some Christians are getting the cart before the horse. They try to be committed to the Lord's work, but they fail because they have not first been fully *converted*. Conversion is essential to total commitment to Christ.

In 1990, center fielder Brett Butler left the San Francisco Giants as a free agent. He was loved in San Francisco, but the best offer came from the L.A. Dodgers—the Giants' rivals. Early in the season, when the two teams met for the first time, Butler was the center of attention. When the announcer read the lineup and introduced the players, the crowd roared as Butler, their former player, was named. The people still loved him; perhaps they thought he was still a Giant at heart. But then Butler did something interesting. When he heard the crowd's response, he walked up to his new manager, Tommy Lasorda, and hugged him. Instantly, the cheers turned to boos and insults. After the game, the press asked him to explain his actions. Butler responded, "It turned a page in my career. I'm an L.A. Dodger now; I'm not a Giant. That just kind of solidified it. I wanted them to know I'm a Dodger."

Perhaps so many Christians are struggling with commitment because they have never fully converted to Christianity. On the outside, they appear to be Christians, but they are still sinners at heart—they are afraid to say, "I'm a Christian now; I'm not a sinner anymore."

Look at the language the New Testament uses of conversion. It speaks in drastic terms. Jesus said, "...Unless you turn ("be converted," KJV) and become like children, you will never enter the kingdom of heaven" (Matthew 18:3). A transformation from a sinful enemy of God (cf. Romans 5:10; James 4:4) to an innocent "child" is noticeable, to say the least. In another place, the Lord explained, "If anyone would come after me, let him deny himself and take up his cross and follow me" (Matthew 16:24). When one understands that the cross in Jesus' day was a symbol of suffering and shame, he recognizes the drastic measures the Lord asked His disciples to take. Paul described conversion in terms of offering oneself up as a "living sacrifice" (Romans 12:1). Similarly, conversion is putting to death or crucifying the old man of sin (Romans 6:3-6; Galatians 2:20). One of the most interesting images describing this particular transformation is that of changing clothes, found in Colossians 3:8-14. Moffatt's translation reads,

But off with them all now, off with anger, rage, malice, slander, foul talk! Tell no lies to one another; you have stripped off the old nature with its practices, and put on the new nature which is renewed in the likeness of its Creator... (vv. 8-10).

One must first *convert* to Christ, and then he can fully *commit* to Him. And what better cause exists? Truly, there is no greater blessing than to be able to serve as a Christian!

A Refusal to Allow Right to Suffer

Generally speaking, righteousness describes a situation where "right" prevails. Unfortunately, some people don't seem bothered when righteousness suffers (cf. Luke 10:30-32). However, David was different. He "stood" for God in that he refused to allow right to suffer!

When David was young, a bold giant named Goliath challenged the army of the Lord's people. Daily, he emerged from the Philistine camp, taunting them:

Why have you come out to draw up for battle? Am I not a Philistine, and are you not servants of Saul? Choose a man for yourselves, and let him come down to me. If he is able to fight with me and kill me, then we will be your servants. But if I prevail against him and kill him, then you shall be our servants and serve us (1 Samuel 17:8-9).

Saul's men were afraid, but David begged the king to let him try his hand with Goliath. David reasoned, "Your servant has struck down both lions and bears, and this uncircumcised Philistine shall be like one of them, for he has defied the armies of the living God" (1 Samuel 17:36). Why was David so passionate? *Goliath had "defied the armies of the living God!"* David loved God, and he loved God's people. It hurt him to see God's cause hurt in any way.

Another illustration of this principle can be found in the fire which was to burn on the altar of the temple of Israel. In Leviticus, the people are commanded, "...It shall not be put out" (6:12, KJV). But in the very next verse, the law says, "Fire shall be kept burning on the altar continually; it shall not go out." In one verse the people were told not to put the fire out, and in the next verse they were told not to let it go out. It would have been just as wrong to let the fire extinguish on its own because of neglect, as it would have been for someone purposely to quench its flame!

This principle is just as true with us. We live in a world and in a time when God's people must take a stand and be counted. Whenever possible, we must prevent God's cause from suffering in any way. David had this spirit. He would not let God's armies be defied. What about you? Are you a defender of God's armies? Can you afford to let right suffer?

Oswald Chambers wrote these inspiring words:

Give me a man of God—one man,
Whose faith is master of his mind,
And I will right all wrongs,
And bless the name of all mankind.

Give me a man of God—one man,
Whose tongue is touched with heaven's fire,
And I will flame the darkest hearts,
With high resolve and clean desire.

Give me a man of God—one man,
One mighty prophet of the Lord,
And I will give you peace on earth,
Bought with a prayer and not a sword.

Give me a man of God—one man,
True to the vision he sees,
And I will build your broken shrines,
And bring the nations to their knees.

God needs "one man"—He needs men and women who will "stand up for Jesus."

Exercises

Fill In The Blanks
1. You have to be certain you are standing for the truth because the world is filled with _____ _____.
2. Jesus' assessment was that the Pharisees' worship was _____.
3. A proper attitude of _____ and _____ for the Creator is behind the faithful men and women of the Old Testament.
4. When Ezra opened the book of the law, all the people _____ _____.
5. Obadiah hid _____ prophets in _____.
6. One must first _____ to Christ, and then he can fully _____ to him.
7. The New Testament's language concerning conversion speaks in _____ terms.
8. Paul described conversion in terms of offering oneself up as a _____ _____.
9. David refused to allow _____ to suffer.
10. Goliath _____ the armies of the living God.

Discussion
1. Explain in your own words what it means to "stand up for Jesus."
2. Making a stand requires a conviction of the truth. What does it take to acquire this conviction (2 Timothy 2:15)?
3. In Romans 11:22, Paul said, "Note then the kindness and the severity of God…." What does this have to do with the subject of reverence?
4. How does God's faithfulness affect our own faithfulness (cf. 2 Timothy 2:13)?
5. Study the attitudes of the priest and the Levite in Luke 10:30-37. How did they differ from the Good Samaritan? Who made a stand based on what was discussed in this lesson?

3
Objections

Maxi Dunnam tells of an interesting ritual practiced by author, Lloyd C. Douglas, during his college years. Downstairs on the first floor of his boarding house lived an elderly, retired music teacher whose health had debilitated to the point that he was unable to leave the apartment. Every morning, Douglas would come down the steps, open the old man's door, and ask, "Well, what's the good news?" The old man would pick up his tuning fork, tap it on the side of his wheelchair, and say, "That's middle C! It was middle C yesterday; it will be middle C tomorrow; it will be middle C a thousand years from now. The tenor upstairs sings flat, the piano across the hall is out of tune, but, my friend, that is middle C!" The old man had taken comfort in a constant while living a life so full of changes.

Americans need to take a cue from an infirmed, retired music teacher and find "middle C." In other words, we must find a body of truth on which we can stand. Too many folks object to this idea. To them, there are no constants, no "middle C's" to reveal what is "out of tune" in life.

In a survey conducted by the Barna Research Group, Americans were asked, "Is there absolute truth?" Amazingly, 66 percent responded that they believe "there is no such thing as absolute truth; different people can define truth in conflicting ways and still be correct." Sadly, the figure rises to 72 percent when it comes to those between the ages of 18 and 25.[4]

Why are so few convinced of real, objective truth? How does a person justify living his life without any constants or standards? Let's consider several objections to making a stand.

"Truth Is a Matter of Opinion."

Many people object to making a stand because they subscribe to a philosophy called "relativism." Relativism basically states that truth is only a matter of opinion and that there are no absolutes. The idea can be summed up in the old adage, "When in Rome, do as the Romans." In other words, if the moral landscape doesn't agree with your convictions, just adapt to fit your surroundings.

What makes relativism so appealing is that it allows one to adjust to the ethics of a particular setting, time, culture, or personality. What if you become good friends with a person and later discover that he likes to get drunk on the weekends? If you are a Christian, there is a problem. When your friend invites you to a wild party, you are going to be forced to confront him. But the relativist doesn't worry about such confrontations. He can adjust. Even if he chooses not to drink, he is not offended when his friend becomes intoxicated. After all, everybody has his own version of right and wrong.

Relativism has been around a long time—even as far back as biblical times. For instance, when Pontius Pilate questioned Jesus during His trials, Jesus told him He came to "bear witness to the truth." He continued, "Everyone who is of the truth listens to my voice." But Pilate was exasperated by the Jews' attempts to convict an innocent man. He was frustrated with Jesus' fixation on the spiritual and His unwillingness to build a defense to save Himself. Thus, in contempt he asked, "What is truth?" His point: Jesus' talk about truth was futile. There is no truth (John 18:37-38).

Absalom was another person who lived by this philosophy. He knew that the people of his day lived by relativism, and so he used it as a tool to win the hearts of Israel and rob his father David of the throne. 2 Samuel 15:6 says that Absalom "stole the hearts of the men of Israel." He would rise early and stand at the city gates, a place where men of prominence would sit and make judgments in civil disputes. He would then wait for those who were coming to the king (his father) for judgment in some matter. When someone would come and relate his problem to the young man, he responded,

> See, your claims are good and right, but there is no man designated by the king to hear you...Oh that I were judge in the land! Then every man with a dispute or cause might come to me, and I would give him justice (2 Samuel 15:3-4).

What Absalom meant was, "Whatever the problem, I will rule in your favor." Because so few of the people really cared about what was actually right and or wrong, this type of dealing won him their favor. However, in the end, all it got him was a violent and shameful death (2 Samuel 18:14).

One cannot harmonize Christianity with relativism because Christianity insists upon actual truth. Jesus said, "And you will know the truth, and the truth will set you free" (John 8:32). He also declared that truth is embodied in God's word (John 17:17). There is a right and there is a wrong, and these are defined in the Bible!

"A Christian Should Never Be Judgmental."

These days the most feared charge that can be lodged against a person in a discussion of any kind is, "You are being judgmental!" For some reason, many folks believe that taking a stand on any issue is harsh and overly critical. In their opinion, all judging is wrong. For this reason, next to John 3:16, Matthew 7:1 is more frequently quoted than any other verse in the Bible: "Judge not, that you be not judged."

Where does this attitude come from? Much of it is rooted in relativism. Because some think that nothing is absolutely right or wrong, they object to any criticism regarding their behavior. Also, our society is marked by a fierce spirit of individualism. People are very protective of their privacy, and they like to govern their own morality. From this vantage point, the church, or any organization for that matter, has no right to intrude into their personal space.

Is it always wrong to be judgmental? No, in fact, it is contradictory to say, "All judging is wrong." Such a statement is a judgment in itself. A person puts himself in a hopeless situation when he tries to claim that *all* judging is wrong.

In Matthew 7:1, when Jesus was instructing us not to make hasty and overly harsh judgments, He was by no means saying that all judging is wrong. In John 7:24, He said, "Do not judge by appearances, but judge with right judgment." We should never criticize others because of how they look or because of an assumption we have made. Instead, we ought to determine what is "right" and critique a person by that standard.

It will not do to object to moral convictions by crying, "You're being judgmental!" There are too many responsibilities given to the Christian which require righteous judgments (cf. Matthew 7:6, 15; Acts 17:11; Galatians 6:1; 2 Timothy 4:2; 1 John 4:1).

"Traditions Can Be Harmful."

Some contend that the moral persuasions based on Christianity are grounded in principles taught a long time ago. They are seen as outdated, irrelevant, tired old traditions that will eventually die with those who defend them. Basically, this is a complaint against anything "traditional."

We must not overlook the truth in this objection. Traditions are beliefs or customs handed down from generation to generation, and sometimes these can be dangerous. Christ Himself warned of how the traditions of man can make worship "vain" (Matthew 15:8-9).

However, not all traditions are harmful. Morals are not outdated if they are grounded in truth. Paul wrote, "So then, brothers, stand firm and hold to the traditions that you were taught by us, either by our spoken word or by our letter" (2 Thessalonians 2:15). Notice here that "traditions" are defined either by the inspired preaching or the inspired writing of the apostles. Paul commanded his readers to "stand firm" in these things. Evidently he did not find them harmful.

So the traditional nature of a practice or belief does not necessarily make it bad. Some things have been done for 2,000 years in the church, and they must continue because they are based on God's pattern found in the New Testament.

"Making a Stand Will Bring Adversity."

This final objection stands unchallenged. There is no denying that a person who defends the truth suffers hardship as a result. But can this fact serve as a reason for not making a stand?

It is interesting that throughout the New Testament, the writers never gloss over the persecution that accompanies the Christian life. Jesus, for example, told His disciples, "If you were of the world, the world would love you as its own; but because you are not of the world, but I chose you out of the world, therefore the world hates you" (John 15:19). Again, in a heartfelt prayer, He said of His disciples, "...the world has hated them because they are not of the world, just as I am not of the world" (John 17:14). Paul proclaimed, "Indeed, all who desire to live a godly life in Christ Jesus will be persecuted" (2 Timothy 3:12). The writer of Hebrews saw this hardship as "the discipline of the Lord" and considered that God "chastises every son whom he receives" (Hebrews 12:5-6). When the Bible speaks on handling tribulation, it never suggests that we should strive against it. Instead, we are told to rejoice because we are able to suffer for the cause of Christ (Acts 5:41; James 1:2-3; 1 Peter 4:12-16).

The apostles never let persecution become an excuse for inaction. When Peter was faced with adversity, he stood for what was right anyway (Acts 4:20).

There is no better example of one who stood in the face of tribulation than Jesus Christ Himself. There is a touching passage in Luke which describes His attitude as He was about to face His opposition in Jerusalem. The Jews would reject Him, His disciples would desert Him, and Judas would betray Him. He would be mocked, spat upon, severely beaten, and, finally, crucified. Yet we read, "When the days drew near for him to be taken up, he set his face to go to Jerusalem" (Luke 9:51).

That kind of resolve is what we need as Christian people today. We need to stop making excuses and make a stand! Only then will we be the kind of disciples Jesus desires.

Now that you know you must take a stand, it's time to take the offensive. Over the next few chapters, we are going to discuss a few battles common to young people. Accordingly, we'll find that a Christian must stand *for* several things.

Exercises

Fill In The Blank
1. _____ percent of Americans said they believed there was no such thing as _____ _____.
2. _____ states that truth is only a matter of opinion.
3. _____ was an Old Testament Bible character who used relativism for evil purposes.
4. Some people believe that taking a stand on anything is being too _____.
5. It is contradictory to say, "All judging is _____."
6. We must judge with _____ judgment.
7. A _____ is a belief or a custom that is handed down from generation to generation.
8. Making a stand will bring _____.
9. The apostles never let _____ become an excuse for inaction.
10. _____ is the greatest example of one who stood in the face of tribulation.
11. All who desire to live a godly life will be _____.
12. Because you are not of the world, the world _____ you.

Discussion
1. Can you think of some ways that relativism affects our society? What are they?
2. What should you say when you are accused of being too judgmental?
3. What are some of the Christian responsibilities that require you to make righteous judgments?
4. Can you think of some traditions we follow in the church? Are these traditions good or bad? How can you know?
5. In what ways are Christians persecuted today in America? What about in other parts of the world?

4 Stand For Your Faith

Polycarp is a name most of you have never heard before. It is the name of a man who took a stand for his faith.

The year was A.D. 156. The dominant empire at that time was Rome. The Caesars who ruled in those days considered themselves to be equal to divinity, and they wanted their citizenry to worship them. Almost everyone responded to these wishes—everyone, that is, except for Christians.

One Christian in particular who did not pay homage to earthly kings was an elder of the church at Smyrna in Asia Minor. At the age of 86, he was one of the wisest, most experienced members of the church. It is likely that he once sat at the feet of the apostle John when he was younger. Later, he became a great leader of the Christian people, and many looked to him for guidance. His name was Polycarp.

During those days, Rome was ruled by bloodthirsty men. If you did not follow Caesar, you were viciously executed for treason. Awful methods of capital punishment were employed in the coliseums. Many were thrown to wild beasts. Others were burned alive at the stake. Because Christians refused to worship Caesar, and because they claimed no king but Christ, they were often subjected to these cruel means of torture.

When Polycarp's Christian influence was discovered

in Asia Minor, he was arrested immediately and sentenced to death by being burned at the stake. Only one thing would save him. He could worship Caesar. Seeing his age, even the Roman authorities pitied him and plead with him to save his life by turning his back on Christ. However, Polycarp replied, "For eighty-six years I have been his servant, and he has done me no wrong. How can I blaspheme my King who saved me?" They continued to insist, saying, "Swear by the Genius (i.e., the guardian spirit) of Caesar," but he persisted by replying,

> Listen carefully: I am a Christian. Now if you want to learn the doctrine of Christianity, name a day and give me a hearing...You threaten with a fire that burns only briefly and after just a little while is extinguished, for you are ignorant of the fire of the coming judgment and eternal punishment, which is reserved for the ungodly. But why do you delay? Come, do what you wish.

At that, his persecutors began preparing a fire. They tied this peaceful, aged Christian to a stake. There, bound as a ram chosen for a burnt offering, he prayed,

> O Lord God Almighty, Father of your beloved and blessed Son Jesus Christ...I bless you because you have considered me worthy of this day and hour, that I might receive a place among the number of the martyrs in the cup of your Christ....

As soon as he said "Amen," the men in charge of the fire lit the wood at his feet, and he was consumed.[5]

What will you do when the time comes for you to take a stand for your faith? Will you be as brave as Polycarp? Maybe the government won't threaten your life, but there will be persecution. Are you strong enough? Is your faith strong enough?

We have already discussed faith as it is used in relation to the gospel (1 Corinthians 16:13). In this sense, faith is the body of truth accepted and followed by a believer. But the word "faith" is used more commonly in another sense to describe one's personal belief. This is the kind of faith that "justifies" Christians (Romans 5:1). Without this faith, it is impossible to please God (Hebrews 11:6). According to James, faith in this sense is "dead" if it is not accompanied by works (2:17). The apostle John stated that this kind of faith is the "victory that has overcome the world" (1 John 5:4). As we discuss standing for your faith in this chapter, keep in mind that we are talking about this personal, inward faith.

What is faith, really? Evidently, there is a lot of confusion over this crucial Christian concept.

Blind Faith

Some take the position that faith is blind. To them, it is based on how you feel, not necessarily on what the facts demonstrate. For example, a person may follow after a particular religion because he "feels" God nudged him in that particular direction. He may not give any other reason for his faith. It is simply a blind trust.

Passages are often quoted in defense of the idea of blind faith, like, "For we walk by faith, not by *sight*" (2 Corinthians 5:7). Or, "Now faith is the assurance of things hoped for, the conviction of things *not seen*" (Hebrews 11:1). Jesus' words to Thomas are cited: "Have you believed because you have seen me? Blessed are those who have *not seen* and yet have believed" (John 20:29). It is true that these verses comment on faith, but they say nothing about "blind faith." They do not rule out *all* lines of evidence, just "sight." Faith can be grounded on other things like logic and inspired testimony. This is exactly what John is trying to tell us in the context of Thomas' belief. After Jesus told the doubting apostle that others would be blessed who believed without seeing Him, John writes,

> Now Jesus did many other signs in the presence of the disciples, which are not written in this book; but these are written so that you may believe that Jesus is the Christ, the Son of God, and that by believing you may have life in his name (John 20:30-31).

John never endorsed blind faith. Instead, he claimed faith should be based upon the inspired word of God! Isn't that exactly what Paul meant when he said, "So faith comes from hearing, and hearing through the word of Christ?" (Romans 10:17).

Borrowed Faith

Another improper development of faith occurs when it is just inherited from another person. This is a common problem among young people. Instead of developing their own faith, they simply borrow it from their parents. At first, it works out nicely. They can be religious, and they can please Mom and Dad without having to do any work. They just copy those who go before them—they go to the same church, sing the same hymns, criticize the same problems, and defend the same traditions. After a while, however, inherited faith fails to sustain its host. You can only survive on someone else's beliefs for a short period of time. When faith is borrowed, it is hollow and cheap.

Jesus taught us that faith is like a mustard seed (Matthew 17:20). The mustard seed is tiny, but after germinating and growing through much care, it turns into a large, tree-like herb. Your faith should be like that little seed. It should grow through much toil, watering, and cultivation, and not through taking someone else's fully-grown tree and planting it in your own yard.

Biblical Faith

Biblical faith is based on evidence. It is not blind or borrowed. That is why it is strong enough to "move mountains."

It would be ridiculous to talk about standing for one's faith if ample evidence did not exist. How can you stand for something that has no proof? Fortunately, plenty of evidence does exist, and because Christians are told to make a defense on behalf of the hope that lies within them (1 Peter 3:15), we will discuss this evidence briefly.

The Law of Cause and Effect

The very fact that something is here is enough to give atheists fits until the end of time. Think about it: If there were ever a time when nothing existed, nothing would exist today. In other words, something cannot come from nothing. This is related to the law of cause and effect.

The law of cause and effect states that every effect must have an adequate cause. If you see a ball rolling, you can safely assume that something caused it to move. While the exact cause may not be certain (e.g., gravity may have pushed it downward, or someone may have rolled it), it does stand to reason that a cause is responsible for its movement. When this is applied to our world, we understand that nothing could exist without a supernatural cause. The cause in this case, of course, is Almighty God. The book of Hebrews puts it this way: "For every house is built by someone, but the builder of all things is God" (3:4).

Design in Nature

Common sense dictates that design indicates a designer. William Paley illustrated this concept using a watch. His reasoning was something like this: Imagine that someone showed you his watch and asked, "Do you think that this watch had an intelligent maker?" You would reply, "Of course, that watch had an intelligent maker." Then suppose I should ask you a second question, "Why do you believe that this watch had an intelligent maker? Did you see the watch being made?" "No," you would respond. Then, he would ask, "How, then, do you know that the watch had an intelligent maker?" You would say, "Everything about it implies intelligent design—its face, the figures on its face in orderly progression, the three hands of the watch revolving so as to mark precisely the time, the battery that powers it, the clasp on the watchband, etc." Then suppose he said, "No, you are mistaken, the watch did not have an intelligent maker. Instead, the wind blew particles around for billions of years until, as a result of a great cosmic accident, out came this watch!" If someone told you that, you would think he was crazy. Why? Because where there is design, there must be a designer.

Everywhere in nature we find beauty, order, law and design. This design conclusively proves the existence of a Designer. The amazing details of the human body, the cyclical movement of water from ocean to clouds to rivers and back to ocean, the photosynthesis of a plant, the intricate relationships between animals and plants in the ecosystem, and many other wonders of nature tell us that God designed them using His divine wisdom (Proverbs 8:22-31). The Psalmist said, "The heavens declare the glory of God, and the sky above proclaims his handiwork" (Psalm 19:1). Paul concurred with that statement, saying that God's "invisible attributes, namely, his eternal power and divine nature, have been clearly perceived, ever since the creation of the world, in the things that have been made..." (Romans 1:20).

Morality

Have you ever wondered why all the civilizations on earth have ruled that murder is wrong? The same is true of stealing, lying, and a number of other crimes. How can the whole world come together in total agreement over fundamental morality? Perhaps it is because God programmed within us a moral sense which tells us the difference between right and wrong.

Unfortunately, history is blighted by the mark left by Adolf Hitler and Nazi Germany. Before the Nazis were defeated, they were able to exterminate millions of Jews in concentration camps. After World War II, they stood trial before the world at Nuremberg. They were charged with cruel and murderous treatment of the Jewish race. But the Nazis denied that these trials were relevant. They argued that their prosecutors were trying them by the laws of a foreign society, and they were only obeying the laws of their own country when they acted to exterminate the Jews. However, they were not excused. They were instead found guilty by a higher law, which, according to R.H. Jackson in his closing address, "rises above the provincial and transient."[6] What law condemned the Nazis? Certainly it was not their own. Also, it was not the United States Constitution or the statutes of Great Britain. Nazi Germany was condemned by a law common to the entire human race, a moral imprint found universally on the human heart.

How can you explain these moral, human instincts without God? If there is no God, what makes murder, rape, robbery, and lying wrong? Isn't "survival of the fittest" the mantra of evolution? Does atheism not promote a life of "every man for himself"? But, generally speaking, the human race doesn't abide by such standards. Instead, we all live by some law that we did not invent and that we know we ought to obey.[7] That law was put there by God.

The apostle Paul wrote of this in his letter to Rome:

> For when Gentiles, who do not have the law, by nature do what the law requires, they are a law to themselves, even though they do not have the law. They show that the work of the law is written on their hearts, while their conscience also bears witness, and their conflicting thoughts accuse or even excuse them (2:14-15).

The Inspiration of the Bible

Let's suppose someone fully believes in God. What then? A simple belief that God exists is not enough to constitute biblical faith. Faith must also be supported by divine revelation.

The Bible claims to be inspired or God-breathed (1 Corinthians 2:13; 2 Timothy 3:16-17; 2 Peter 1:20-21). Can we be sure of the validity of this claim? Consider the following:
- Although the Bible was penned over a period of about 1,400 years by about 40 different men, it is a work of complete harmony. Its unity is unquestionable.
- The Bible is not a textbook on science, but whenever it incidentally mentions scientific facts, it does so with amazing accuracy (cf. Job 38:16; Psalm 8:8; Isaiah 40:22).
- The Bible doesn't contradict historical facts. For example, in the book of Acts, Luke mentions 32 countries, 54 cities, and nine Mediterranean islands. He also mentions 95 persons, 62 of which are not named elsewhere in the New Testament. All of these references have been shown to be completely accurate, where it is possible to check them.[8]
- Also, the Bible has proven itself to be flawlessly accurate in the matter of predictive prophecy. Consider, as just one example, the predictions regarding the life of Christ (Psalm 16:8-10; 22;

41:9; Isaiah 7:14; 53; Micah 5:2; Zechariah 11:12-13; et al.).

All of this evidence conclusively presents a factual basis for our faith. There is no reason to rely on blind or borrowed faith. Plenty of proof abounds.

Maybe you won't have to suffer like Polycarp, but your faith will be challenged. Prepare yourself so that you can stand for your faith!

Exercises

Fill In The Blanks
1. _____ was an elder of the church at Smyrna in Asia Minor.
2. The word "faith" is most often used to describe one's _____ _____.
3. Sometimes passages are quoted in defense of _____ _____ (2 Corinthians 5:7; Hebrews 11:1; John 20:29).
4. Faith should be based on the _____ word of God.
5. Some people _____ faith from their parents.
6. Faith is like a _____ seed.
7. If there were ever a time when nothing existed, _____ would exist today.
8. The law of cause and effect states that every _____ must have an adequate _____.
9. Design indicates a _____.
10. God programmed within us a _____ sense which tells us the difference between right and wrong.
11. The Bible was written over a period of _____ years by about _____ different men, and yet it is a complete work of harmony.

Discussion
1. If you lived in the days of Polycarp, what kinds of things would you do to withstand persecution?
2. What can a young person do to avoid borrowed faith?
3. What can a young person do to avoid blind faith?
4. Study what the Bible says about the human conscience (Acts 23:1; Romans 2:14-15; 1 Timothy 4:1-2; 1 Peter 3:21; et al.). How does this relate to the moral law?

5 Stand For Yourself

In the last chapter, we addressed the most important place to make your stand: your personal faith in God. Without this conviction, you cannot possibly begin to live the Christian life. Every aspect of Christianity—worship, service, beliefs, etc.—is based upon a persuasion that there is one God and that He sent His Son Jesus to rid the world of sin.

Let's go one step further. We have already noticed that faith in God is the most important thing. What comes next? If *faith in God* is the most important thing, then next in importance is *faith in yourself*. That is why in this chapter we are going to discuss some keys to building a healthy self-esteem.

Basically, self-esteem denotes a feeling of self-worth. When it is high, it emboldens an individual to take on challenges and soar to new heights. When it is low, it leads to a lack of commitment, depression, negligence, and irresponsible behavior. Unfortunately, many Christians are plagued with a low self-esteem that holds them back from being hard-working, dedicated, happy people.

The Christian life is not easy. In fact, Jesus described the "gate" to this kind of life as "strait" (Matthew 7:13-14, KJV). The word "strait" (not "straight") indicates a portal that is narrow and navigable with some degree of difficulty. Maybe you have studied the "Strait of Magellan" in school. It is a narrow, difficult waterway that weaves through the southern tip of the continent of South America. The gate by which Christians must enter eternal life is like that narrow, twisting waterway—it is "strait" and filled with many challenges. That fact is made clear in many places in the Bible (Mark 10:28-30; John 15:18-21; 16:33; Acts 14:22; 1 Thessalonians 3:3; 2 Timothy 3:12). Since this is the case, how can a Christian possibly face the difficulties before him with a low self-esteem? We need to develop a healthy sense of self-worth so that we can make our stand.

An Inferiority Complex

Before we get into some keys to building a healthy self-esteem, let's consider one particularly common manifestation of low self-esteem: the inferiority complex.

Humility is a Christian virtue. In Romans 12:3, Paul said, "For by the grace given to me I say to everyone among you not to think of himself more highly than he ought to think…." But if what Paul said is true, then wouldn't the opposite apply as well? We should not think "more highly" of ourselves than we ought to think, but we should not think "more lowly" of ourselves either!

Sometimes a problem with self-esteem is exhibited through an "inferiority complex." Simply put, a person with this problem feels like he is lower in quality than other people. Consequently, a person struggling with feelings of inferiority often feels depressed and worthless. This is not a new problem. In fact, it can even be traced back to biblical times.

In Paul's first letter to the church at Corinth, we find that at least some of his readers were struggling with an inferiority complex. This should be no surprise. The city of Corinth itself was a competitive place. Every other year, people would come to Corinth to see the Isthmian Games, a competition similar to our Olympic Games. Here, athletes would showcase their impressive talents. Also, the city's strategic location on the Greek peninsula made it a busy center of commerce. This made it an attractive location for wealthy business owners. Furthermore, Corinth was the seat of government for the Roman province of Achaia. That introduced a political climate filled with statesmen and officials, all vying for the highest position.

The Corinthian church, it seems, was also a place where people were constantly being compared to see who was "best." This was the age of miracles, and many members of the church possessed impressive gifts. Some could heal the sick. Others could prophesy. There were some who could speak in tongues, and then there were others who interpreted the tongues (cf. 1 Corinthians 12:8-10). Picture yourself as a member of that congregation. What if your particular gift was not as prominent as someone else's? Better yet, what if you did not even have a spiritual gift? What if you possessed only natural talents and abilities? How would you feel? Apparently, some of the Corinthians in those days felt inferior.

In Paul's letter to this congregation, he tried to help those struggling with an inferiority complex by discussing "feet" and "ears." He had been illustrating the unity of the church using the human body. Notice what he says in 1 Corinthians 12:12: "For just as the body is one and has many members, and all the members of the body, though many, are one body, so it is with Christ." His point was that the body is not composed of members all possessing the same function, but rather it has many different members—fingers, toes, eyes, ears, a nose, hair, skin, etc.—and these all work together in a unified, cohesive way. Then he came to the "feet" and the "ears":

> If the foot should say, "Because I am not a hand, I do not belong to the body," that would not make it any less a part of the body. And if the ear should say, "Because I am not an eye, I do not belong to the body," that would not make it any less a part of the body. If the whole body were an eye, where would be the sense of hearing? If the whole body were an ear, where would be the sense of smell? (1 Corinthians 12:15-17).

Your feet and your ears are not the most attractive parts of your body. In fact, to be brutally honest, they are really pretty ugly! But they perform very important functions. For this reason, Paul used them to illustrate the situation of those who were feeling inferior. Maybe they didn't have the most exciting gift. Maybe their particular talent wasn't all that sensational. Maybe they were just an ugly old "foot" or an unsightly "ear." That didn't matter. They were still important to the body. Later on the apostle writes, "The eye cannot say to the hand, 'I have no need of you,' nor again the head to the feet, 'I have no need of you.' On the contrary, the parts of the body that seem to be weaker are indispensable..." (1 Corinthians 12:21-22). "Indispensable." That's what you are no matter what part of the body you represent!

    Every member is important, and we can't all perform the same function. Some of us will be preachers, and some of us will mow the yard. Some of us will teach Bible classes, and others will be encouragers like Barnabas. But everybody is important. In fact, Paul claimed that we are who we are because God made us that way. Look at verse 18 of the text we have been studying: "But as it is, God arranged the members in the body, each one of them, as he chose." Let's not complain, then, because somebody can excel in an area where we struggle. Instead, we ought to look for the special talents and abilities we possess and use them. God has arranged you in your own special place in the body of Christ, and He wants you to do the best you can with what you have. He has a plan for you. You are important!

Keys to Building a Healthy Self-Esteem

How can I overcome my inferiority complex? How can I defeat a low self-esteem? Here are six keys to help you build a healthy self-esteem.

Key #1: Balance your self-esteem with humility.

Notice that we are building a "healthy" self-esteem, and not necessarily a "high" self-esteem. We have already said that humility is a Christian virtue (Ephesians 4:1-3; Philippians 2:2-4). Thus, it is important that we balance our good self-esteem with a sense of humility.

Too often, people think that having a mind intoxicated with pride is the same as possessing a good self-esteem. The writers of the New Testament employed an interesting term to describe those under this impression. The King James Version translates it "vain glory" (Galatians 5:26; Philippians 2:3). The term denotes somebody who has an opinion of himself which is empty, vain, or false. In actuality the perception of a vainglorious person is all wrong—it is simply an illusion about himself to hide the truth because he is uncomfortable with reality.[9] The key is to "think with sober judgment" (Romans 12:3) and form a humble opinion of yourself.

It is wrong to think that humility is the opposite of a positive self-esteem. In fact, the two work hand in hand. Humility prevents an individual from forming unrealistic expectations for himself and later becoming frustrated when he is unable to perform.

I remember an episode of the *Andy Griffith Show* entitled "A Medal for Opie" that well illustrates how humility is helpful in preventing us from becoming exasperated by disappointments. In this particular episode, Opie wants to enter a footrace. Barney decides that he is going to be the boy's personal trainer and boosts his ego. Pretty soon, in Opie's mind, there is no way he is going to lose that race. His father keeps telling him that there is a chance he won't win, but Opie doesn't listen. His mind is made up. When the day of the race comes, Opie races, but he doesn't win. In fact, he comes in last place. Instead of congratulating the winner and going on to enjoy the rest of the day, he goes off to sulk in his own misery. Why couldn't the young boy handle his defeat? Because he was too puffed up with pride! He failed to "think with sober judgment."

Humility can help us set realistic goals and face life's little disappointments. We need to feel able to accomplish great things, but we also need to realize that we can't always be winners.

Key #2: Fight negative influences.

Young people often develop their opinions about themselves from the way they are viewed by the people around them. If these influences are negative, then they could have a devastating effect upon a fragile, impressionable mind. What makes these influences difficult to ignore is the fact that they often come from loved ones, like a parent or a friend. One woman named Betty spoke of her struggle with low self-esteem, saying,

> My experience with the things that caused me to have low self-esteem is what my mother did to me. She made me feel bad about myself. I never did anything right...If there was a way of laying a guilt trip on me for failing at something, she could do it! I didn't find out that I was smart and had any strengths until I became an adult.[10]

Unfortunately, some parents do a lot of damage to their children's feelings of self-worth. This is a sad but obvious truth.

So what can be done? To develop a healthy self-esteem, we must fight the negative influences that assail us. For the Christian, this challenge is heightened because the world hates him (John 15:19). Therefore, you have to be fiercely independent in developing your sense of self-worth. Fight those negative influences!

Key #3: Realize your value as a human being.

If you want to feel valuable, read the Bible. According to inspiration, every human being is priceless. Reflect upon the following information:
- Every person is made in the image of God (Genesis 1:26-27).
- Human beings possess an immortal soul that will live forever (Ecclesiastes 12:7).
- Every individual is loved by God (John 3:16).
- Christ died for each individual person (notice the personal pronoun "me" in Galatians 2:20).
- Although every person sins and alienates himself from God (Romans 3:23), God wants to save him (1 Timothy 2:3-4).
- The angels in heaven rejoice over one sinner that repents (Luke 15:10).
- The Father Himself rejoices over one sinner that repents (Luke 15:20; 2 Peter 3:9).

What are you worth? The Bible says you are valuable beyond comprehension!

Your value is compounded when you become a Christian, for at that point, you become a child and an heir of God (Romans 8:15-17; Galatians 3:28-29).

Key #4: Base your self-esteem upon something real.

Over the last thirty years, schools have recognized the importance of a good self-esteem. A correlation has been discovered between this and performance in school children. Accordingly, parents and teachers have striven to boost self-esteem. However, their methodology has been flawed. Too often, the goal has been the high self-esteem itself, rather than the success that properly leads to a high self-esteem.

A *Wall Street Journal* article reported on this problem by describing how a professor sent an email containing a review question to students who had done poorly on an exam. The question was intended to prepare the students for a make-up test. Within this message, the instructor embedded a little experiment. To a third of the group, he sent advice to study harder. But to another third, he sent a pep talk aimed at raising their self-esteem, something like, "You're too smart to get a D!" Can you guess who did better on the make-up test? The ones who received the pep talk did notably worse than those who were encouraged to study harder and achieve more.[11] The point is that studies prove that it takes more than a pep talk to really raise a person's self-esteem. To get results, one must base his self-esteem upon something real.

This is the point Paul is trying to make in Galatians 6. In verse 3, he says, "For if anyone thinks he is something, when he is nothing, he deceives himself." He is still correcting those who were struggling with "vain glory" (cf. Galatians 5:26). They have built an illusion of themselves, and Paul is trying to tear it down for them. But if that false perception is removed, what will happen to the person's self-esteem? It will crumble if the vain glory is not replaced with something legitimate. So, instead of simply giving them a pep talk with nothing behind it (i.e., "You're too good to go to hell!"), Paul encourages them to excel: "But let each one test his own work, and then his reason to boast will be in himself alone and not in his neighbor. For each will have to bear his own load" (vv. 4-5). Paul realized that it takes more than pep talks to promote a healthy self-esteem. Therefore, he encouraged Christians to "bear their own load." That is, he asked them to use their talents to do what they could do for the cause of Christ. After all, on Judgment Day, God is not going to look at the size of your self-esteem. Instead, "each will have to bear his own load." In other words, you will be judged based upon what you have done, not on how great other people have made you out to be (Philippians 2:12; Romans 14:12; 2 Corinthians 5:10).

Self-esteem ought to be based upon something real if it is going to bear positive results. But someone might object by saying, "What if I'm not particularly talented? What if success doesn't come all that easily to me?" Well, if we define success as the world does—in achieving great athletic feats, for example, or having sex appeal—then most of us will never excel. Some of us are just not able to attain that kind of success.

Young people struggling with low self-esteem need to shift their desire from worldly success to spiritual success. Spiritual success is challenging but attainable by all, regardless of attractiveness or abilities. Also, spiritual success will provide richer rewards (Matthew 6:19-21; 1 Peter 1:3-4). All of us can excel by God's standards, and we ought to use this kind of achievement to boost our self-esteem.

Key #5: Be the captain of your own ship.

Whenever you let someone else make all the decisions regarding your life, your feeling of self-worth is going to diminish. It is important that we listen to good advice, but in the end, we should make our own decisions. This gives us a sense of independence and makes us feel like a person instead of a robot following instructions.

Whenever we make our own decisions, however, we need to remember to put Christ first (Matthew 6:33; 2 Corinthians 10:5). Ultimately, He should be the true "captain of our ship."

Key #6: Tap into your own special talents.

Anita Roddick said, "If you think you're too small to make a difference, you haven't been in bed with a mosquito." A mosquito, though very small, can get a lot of attention. But why? It is because he utilizes his unique ability. If all a mosquito ever did was buzz around, it would hardly be noticeable. However, when it applies that unique mouth to our skin and sucks our blood, we take notice!

Remember what Paul told the Corinthians. You are a part of the body of Christ, and God has determined a special purpose for you by the natural talents and abilities He has given you. Don't overlook them. They are there. And you must develop them and use them for His glory.

Stand for God, but also stand for yourself. Without a healthy self-esteem, you will achieve very little, if anything at all, in the kingdom of God.

Exercises

Fill In The Blanks
1. Christians must enter a _____ gate.
2. A common manifestation of low self-esteem is the _____ _____.
3. The city of Corinth was a _____ place.
4. God _____ the members in the body as He _____.
5. _____ and a healthy self-esteem work hand in hand.
6. Young people often develop their opinions about themselves from the way they are _____ by the people around them.
7. Every person is made in the _____ of God.
8. Human beings possess an immortal _____.
9. The Father _____ over one sinner that repents.
10. Paul encouraged Christians to _____ their own load.
11. To develop a positive self-esteem, you must develop your _____ and use them for God's glory.

Discussion
1. What are some characteristics of a person who suffers from a low self-esteem?
2. How do the "feet" and "ears" of the body illustrate the situation of church members who feel inferior to others?
3. What is the difference between a "healthy" self-esteem and a "high" self-esteem?
4. How do you balance making your own decisions with listening to the advice of others?
5. How can a person discover his talents?

6
Stand For The Truth

No one stood for God's word like the apostle Paul. In his words, he was "put here for the defense of the gospel" (Philippians 1:16; cf. v. 7). This was his purpose in life. In what seemed like another lifetime, he was Saul, the persecutor of the church. But on one unforgettable day, when he was on the road to Damascus, Christ upset his life and picked him to be "a chosen instrument" to bring the gospel to "Gentiles and kings and the children of Israel" (Acts 9:15). From that day forward, Paul became a fierce defender of the gospel.

As he mentored the young man Timothy, the apostle sought to encourage his apprentice to make the same stand. "Preach the word," he wrote, "be ready in season and out of season; reprove, rebuke, and exhort, with complete patience and teaching" (2 Timothy 4:2). The language Paul used to tell Timothy to "be ready" is interesting. It was often used to describe a sudden appearance, such as the time an angel suddenly appeared and stood next to Peter in his prison cell (Acts 12:7). The older evangelist was telling his younger counterpart to "stand by," to be ready to preach the word whenever the occasion called for it. This may be "in season," when times are favorable to preaching the word, or it may be "out of season," when speaking up could be quite dangerous.

The stance Paul required of Timothy is reflected in one of Peter's letters:

But in your hearts regard Christ the Lord as holy, always being prepared to *make a defense* to anyone who asks you for a reason for the hope that is in you; yet do it with gentleness and respect, having a good conscience, so that, when you are slandered, those who revile your good behavior in Christ may be put to shame (1 Peter 3:15-16).

Peter, like Paul and Timothy, was set to defend the gospel with all of his might.

Why were these men so protective of God's word? There are a lot of good books out there. We are not called on to die for any of these. What makes the gospel so special? The answer is really quite simple. It is special because it is "truth" (John 17:17).

Before we consider the significance of truth, we need to think about another question: How can I really know that the Bible fully embodies truth? How is it possible for a bundle of paper, ink, and glue to be so valuable?

The Bible is special because it is the only book that is "inspired." The word "inspired" simply means "God-breathed." We read, "All Scripture is breathed out by God and profitable for teaching, for reproof, for correction, and for training in righteousness, that the man of God may be competent, equipped for every good work" (2 Timothy 3:16-17). This indeed is an intriguing statement because we know that scripture was originally penned by human beings; it didn't just appear out of thin air (cf. Jeremiah 45:1; Luke 1:1-4; Revelation 1:9-11). How can we call the Bible "inspired" if it was written down in the same manner as every other book?

Evidently, the Bible was breathed out by God through some miraculous process involving both God and men. While much of this remains a mystery to us, some amazing clues are revealed for our enlightenment.

First of all, the Holy Spirit served as the agent of the inspiration process. Whenever we read of someone speaking or writing the words of God, they do so "by" the Holy Spirit (2 Samuel 23:2; John 14:26; 16:13; Acts 1:16; 2 Peter 1:20-21). Secondly, we can understand that as the Holy Spirit taught men things to speak and write, He did so in *words*, not thoughts or intimations. For instance, Paul said that the inspired words he was speaking and writing came "not in words taught by human wisdom, but in those taught by the Spirit, combining spiritual thoughts with spiritual words" (1 Corinthians 2:13, NASB). Thirdly, not *some* but *all* of scripture is inspired in this manner (2 Timothy 3:16). Therefore, one should not pick and choose some things out of the Bible and apply them to his life. *All* of it is important.

From what has been revealed to us about the inspiration process, we can conclude the following:
- God's word is not merely the product of human genius. It rises above the level of the works of Shakespeare or the Constitution of the United States.
- God did not inspire the thoughts of men but the words. This is an important fact when you consider that the writers could have easily made mistakes in transferring inspired thoughts into their own words.
- We cannot conclude that only part of Scripture is inspired. Every word, from Genesis to Revelation, has been revealed by God.
- God's word is fully inspired in a word-for-word fashion.

With this amazing inspiration process in mind, and having the assurance that God's word embodies absolute truth, let's turn to the challenge of this lesson: *stand for the truth.*

Jesus gave His disciples a motive for standing for the truth when He said, "You will know the truth, and the truth will set you free" (John 8:32). Freedom. That's why you ought to make a stand for God's word. The Bible, unlike all other books, has the power to liberate you!

Freedom From Sin

The immediate context of Jesus' statement, "The truth will make you free," addresses the oppression of sin. Two verses later, He says, "Truly, truly, I say to you, everyone who commits sin is a slave to sin" (John 8:34). How true. Ask any sinner who is honest with himself, and he will tell you that he is a slave. The compulsive gambler, the adulterer, the robber, the liar, the gossip, the alcoholic—all of them must admit that they are trapped in oppression. "For whatever overcomes a person, to that he is enslaved" (2 Peter 2:19).

The dangerous thing about the slavery of sin is that, after a while, it can get comfortable. People bound in the chains of iniquity often become blinded to the danger of their imprisonment. Not long ago, a reintroduction program went awry when a California condor that had been released into the wild kept walking up to people and allowing them to pick him up. This giant bird, with a wingspan of nearly ten feet, had become accustomed to captivity and didn't want to go back into the wild.[12] Slavery had grown on him. That bird was meant to soar through the western skies, to perch atop mountains, and scavenge the canyons for food. But instead he was a canary in a cage. Captivity had blinded him from seeing his true potential. That same blindness overcomes the individual trapped in sin. Because he lets his fleshly lusts and the darkness of the world direct his life, he lives a lie. And the longer he continues in the lie, the closer he comes to death.

The truth revealed in God's word can free you from all the lies. It exposes sin as deadly (Romans 6:23;

Ephesians 2:1), and it illuminates the pathway to life (John 6:68; Philippians 2:15; 2 Timothy 1:10; 1 John 1:1). Thus, it follows that freedom from sin also means freedom from death. Of course, truth cannot release you from physical death; all of us must die (Hebrews 9:27). However, a far greater death than the physical kind is caused by sin: *spiritual death*. Many people think of death in terms of an end. But actually death is separation. When someone physically dies, their spirit is separated from their body (James 2:26). Likewise, whenever one dies spiritually, he is separated from God (Isaiah 59:1-2). If one does not find the truth, and he fails to learn to escape death through the blood of Christ, the separation becomes eternal in the afterlife, and the prospect of freedom at this point is hopeless! (Luke 16:19-31; Revelation 21:8).

Freedom From Falsehood

"Beware of false prophets," Jesus said, "who come to you in sheep's clothing but inwardly are ravenous wolves" (Matthew 7:15). It is easy to get caught in the trap of falsehood because those who promote it are good at what they do. The Lord used an interesting illustration to warn His disciples of the disguise of a false teacher. "Sheep's clothing" suggests that this disguise is *comforting*. The sheep is the animal used to represent Christ Himself (Isaiah 53:7; John 1:29; 1 Peter 1:18-19). Also, His followers are called the "flock of God" (Acts 20:28-29). This meek animal is a fitting symbol of Christianity because it is gentle, innocent, and pure. That is exactly why a false prophet wears its clothing. He wants a comforting costume that will draw people into his confidence.

Not only is the disguise of sheep's clothing *comforting*, but it is also *convincing*. In the past, when I read this verse I would imagine the Big Bad Wolf in Saturday morning cartoons, stalking sheep and hiding behind a sheep's pelt that only partially covered him. I always looked at him and wondered how those sheep could be fooled into thinking he was a real sheep. But the word Christ uses in this instance does not denote a pelt but all that the sheep have on. Thus, He is saying the propagators of falsehood have the very appearance of sheep.[13] In other places in the New Testament, similar references are made to the clever concealment of false prophets (Matthew 24:23-24; 2 Corinthians 11:13-15). Indeed, their disguise is both *comforting* and *convincing*.

In reality, they are nothing but ravenous wolves. Read some of the things the Bible says about wolves (Genesis 49:27; Ezekiel 22:27; Habakkuk 1:8; Zephaniah 3:3; Matthew 10:16; John 10:12; Acts 20:28-30). Their intentions are never good. They have ravenous appetites for the souls of men; they seek to shed blood and destroy souls; and they will resort to anything in order to gratify their evil cravings. The Lord uses this language of false teachers because He wants us to know that they are extremely dangerous.

The only thing that can cure falsehood is truth. After Jesus warned of wolves in sheep's clothing, he said, "You will recognize them by their fruits" (Matthew 7:16). Refuse to blindly accept a teacher without considering his credentials. Look at his doctrine. Consider his conduct. Are these consistent with Christ's sayings and actions? If not, you have a false prophet on your hands. He is a ravenous wolf, and he wants to do you harm. It doesn't matter how cleverly he has disguised himself. He may appear to be an angel of light, but if he does not speak the truth and you follow him anyway, he will be the source of your destruction! Follow truth. It will lead you away from false teachers.

Freedom From Uncertainty

Ever since scientists successfully cloned the first large animal, a sheep named Dolly, the whole world entered into a raging debate over the ethics of cloning human beings.

In the midst of all this hubbub, a strange religious group called the Raelians claimed that their organization, aptly named Clonaid, had successfully cloned the first human baby, a little girl named Eve. At first, this group attracted a lot of media attention, but soon a number of things surfaced causing many people to question their credibility. When asked how they came to be the first to achieve this scientific breakthrough, the Raelians claimed they used knowledge supplied by space aliens. Apparently, they believe that the earth was colonized by cloned humans left behind by extraterrestrial beings who visited the earth from a distant part of the galaxy. Furthermore, they say their plans are eventually to perpetuate individuals by creating adult clones and downloading memories and personality into the new, identical bodies. In this manner they would, in their own words, create immortal beings whose bodies would be regularly replaced by clones. These strange claims coupled with absolutely no proof of cloning capability led the public to dismiss their announcement as an elaborate hoax.

The Raelians are an extreme example, but we are faced daily with people making new claims. Muslims claim that Islam is the true religion; Jews preach the Torah. Atheists argue against any religion whatsoever. According to them, evolution is the explanation behind our universe. Who is right? How can anyone be certain of anything in this world?

Truth will free you from uncertainty. It can be used either to confirm or deny the validity of a claim. But assurance only comes to those who are willing to study the truth and use it to examine the claims. The Bereans serve as a good example for us to follow. Even when the apostle Paul preached, they examined "the Scriptures daily to see if these things were so" (Acts

17:11). John said, "Beloved, do not believe every spirit, but test the spirits to see whether they are from God, for many false prophets have gone out into the world" (1 John 4:1).

"You will know the truth, and the truth will set you free." Because truth has the power to set us free, we must stand for it! Otherwise, all is lost.

Exercises

Fill In The Blanks
1. Christ picked Paul to be a chosen _____.
2. Paul told Timothy, "Preach the word, _____ _____ in season and out of season..." (2 Timothy 4:2).
3. Peter said we must always be prepared to make a _____ to anyone who asks for a reason for the hope that is in us (1 Peter 3:15).
4. The Bible is the only book that is _____.
5. The _____ _____ served as the agent of the inspiration process.
6. When the Holy Spirit taught men things to speak and write, He did so in _____, not _____.
7. God's word embodies absolute _____.
8. "You will know the _____, and the _____ will set you _____" (John 8:32).
9. After a while, the slavery of sin can get _____.
10. Truth exposes sin as _____.
11. The disguises of false teachers can be both _____ and _____.
12. The _____ serve as a good example of a group of people who searched the scriptures to free themselves from uncertainty.

Discussion
1. After it is concluded that the Bible is inspired, a number of implications follow. Can you name some of them?
2. What are some ways that sin enslaves people today?
3. Do we consider false teachers to be "ravenous wolves" (Matthew 7:15)? How should we respond to false teachers? (cf. 2 Timothy 4:2; 2 John 9-11).
4. What is wrong with uncertainty? Why should we be certain of the truth?

7 Stand For Worship

When Abraham worshipped, his sacrifices were full of meaning. His heart was full of reverence and devotion for his God as he turned to his servants in the land of Moriah and said, "I and the boy will go over there and worship..." (Genesis 22:5). This had been a response to a command the Lord had given him. Abraham, the would-be father of a nation, was to take his only son Isaac and offer him as a burnt offering. Rising early in the morning, he loaded firewood on his donkey, packed a knife, and began the long ascent up the mountain chosen by God. Isaac's only inquiry concerned the absence of a lamb for the sacrifice. His father replied, "God will provide for himself the lamb for a burnt offering, my son." Then the two of them kept climbing in silence.

It is hard to imagine what might have been going on in Abraham's mind when he took the knife to slaughter his son. The writer of the book of Hebrews gives us a clue: "He considered that God was able even to raise him from the dead..." (11:19). But before Abraham's knife was able to find its target, God's intentions were made clear. It was a test. Seeing that His servant Abraham succeeded, God commended him, saying, "Now I know that you fear God, seeing you have not withheld your son, your only son, from me" (Genesis 22:12). Suddenly, there appeared a ram, caught in a thicket by his horns. As faithful Abraham expected, the Lord had indeed provided, and even unto the time of Moses' recording the incident in the book of Genesis, that place was known by the name Abraham gave it that day: "The Lord Will Provide."

Do you think Abraham's experience in the land of Moriah was meaningful? To say that Abraham would remember that incident for the rest of his life is an understatement. It was a time when the providence of God was forever stamped on the old patriarch's mind.

David was another Old Testament character who took his worship seriously. Consider a sampling of his statements in the Psalms:

Bless the Lord, O my soul! O Lord my God, you are very great! You are clothed with splendor and majesty...I will sing to the Lord as long as I live; I will sing praise to my God while I have being...Praise the Lord, all nations! Extol him, all peoples! For great is his steadfast love toward us, and the faithfulness of the Lord endures forever. Praise the Lord! ...Praise the Lord from the heavens; praise him in the heights! Praise him, all his angels; praise him, all his hosts! Praise him, sun and moon, praise him, all you shining stars! Praise him, you highest heavens, and you waters above the heavens! (104:1, 33; 117; 148:1-4).

The apostles valued worship so much that they risked their lives in order to visit the temple in Jerusalem, where their enemies often awaited them. A trip to the temple at the hour of prayer landed Peter and John in prison and on trial before the Council (Acts 3-4). Likewise, when Paul entered the temple to fulfill a vow, his opponents took advantage of the situation and arrested him (Acts 21:26ff.).

Obviously, men like Abraham, David, Peter, John, and Paul viewed worship as an honor, a privilege! Contrast their attitude with a disturbing mind-set common among worshippers today. Unfortunately, many perceive worship to be a boring chore, a duty to be fulfilled at the beginning of every week. This sentiment is not unlike that of the Jews in Malachi's day, who "snorted" and said, "What a weariness this is!" (Malachi 1:13). Far too many have made worship a low priority. Some people, who seem to have been dragged to church kicking and screaming, look bored and glum as they worship. Even young people, who are still living under the care and guidance of their parents, take jobs that will prevent them from attending the services of the church.

Can worship have as much meaning to us as it did to Abraham and David? It can if we get back to the fundamentals revealed in the Bible. The one who applies these to his heart will find that worship is not merely a duty; it is a privilege!

An Explanation of Worship

If you listen to many commercials promoting religious groups on the radio or television, you will hear the same words associated with worship over and over again: "entertaining," "inclusive," "come as you are," "uplifting," "invigorating," "relevant," "comfortable." However, none of these fully explains the true meaning of worship.

The most common word used for worship in the New Testament literally means to "kiss toward." Originally, it signified the way a worshipper in ancient times would kiss a hand or feet or the ground out of devotion to someone or something. This usually involved bowing low with the face to the ground. Later the focus of the word moved from external bowing and kissing to an internal "bowing" of the heart. So basically, in the New Testament, the most common word for worship refers to acts of reverence paid to God.

Jesus referred to the "bowing" of the heart when He

said, "God is spirit, and those who *worship* him must *worship* in spirit and truth" (John 4:24, emphasis added). In making this statement, the Lord limited worship to two distinct realms. First of all, worship must be conducted in "spirit," or sincerely and from the heart. Secondly, worship must be done in "truth." This means that it must be authorized by God in His word. One cannot eliminate either of these elements and expect God to accept his worship. In fact, it is possible to sit in a church assembly and yet fail to worship properly. If a person worships without the right "spirit" or outside the realm of "truth," he should not expect God to be satisfied.

Thus, worship can be explained as acts of reverence paid to God, which fall into both the categories of "spirit" and "truth." This being the case, three important conclusions follow.

1. Worship requires *preparation*. Saturday night has become the night to go out and have a good time. On the weekends, we go to bed late and wake up late the following morning. Consequently, people are getting to worship services late and unprepared, with harried expressions on their faces.

An alertness and calm focus is necessary to perform acts of worship. In order to achieve this state of mind, one must prepare. This includes getting plenty of rest, reading and meditating upon God's word sometime prior to services, and planning ahead to avoid anything that will distract you from giving full devotion to God.

2. Worship requires *panting*. That doesn't mean you should come to church out of breath, with your tongue hanging out of your mouth. "Panting" means one should have a spiritual appetite that leads him to worship. David said, "As a deer pants for flowing streams, so pants my soul for you, O God. My soul thirsts for God, for the living God. When shall I come and appear before

God?" (Psalm 42:1-2).

Your heart will never "bow" to God until it yearns to appear before His throne as intensely as a parched mouth yearns for water. As Jesus said, "Blessed are those who hunger and thirst for righteousness, for they shall be satisfied" (Matthew 5:6). Developing that kind of an appetite requires patience and training. Many worldly influences work to build sinful appetites. The Christian must work to build a spiritual appetite by feeding on a spiritual diet. After all, your appetite is shaped by your diet (Matthew 4:4).

3. Worship requires *participation*. Worship begins inwardly in the heart. Upon learning this, some may get the idea that it is passive, not requiring much participation at all. Nothing could be further from the truth! Our culture has conditioned us to become entertainment-oriented. Thus, we are often guilty of showing up for worship, taking our pew, and waiting to be entertained. Then if we are not uplifted, it is not our fault. We blame the song leader or the preacher. But worship is not a spectator sport. It requires participation. Throughout the Bible, the responsibility for uplifting worship rests upon the individual worshippers, not just the man leading in worship.

The End Of Worship

Not only did Jesus explain worship to us in John 4:24, but He also revealed the end or object of true worship: "*God* is spirit, and those who worship him must worship in spirit and truth." If worship is going to be meaningful, it must be focused in the right direction—towards God (Matthew 4:9-10; Philippians 3:3).

There should be no doubt in our minds that God is worthy of such adoration. All of us should take a cue from the four living creatures described in Revelation 4, who day and night ceased not to say, "Holy, holy, holy, is the Lord God Almighty, who was and is and is to come!"

It is painfully clear that the rightful end of worship has been neglected in many places. Entertainment dominates the assembly halls of popular religion. Instruments of music ring loudly, though God never ordained them for Christian worship. Theatrical performances replace biblical preaching. Soloists perform before a crowd of admiring listeners. Some are even turning their worship services into a banquet, where food and drinks are served (cf. 1 Corinthians 11:20-22)! These practices represent a backwards perspective on worship. Those engaged in them are not considering what God wants out of worship; they are more interested in what *they* want. They worship, but they do so in vain (Matthew 15:8-9).

The Expressions Of Worship

As it was explained earlier, true worship begins internally. It is a "bowing" of the heart. That internal bowing, however, must be outwardly expressed.

Is it up to us to discover the best ways to express the adoration and praise that resides in our hearts? Remember that the end of our worship is God. So whatever expression is used ought to be pleasing to Him. Otherwise, we defeat the purpose. Also, it is helpful to realize that God's ways are entirely different from our own (1 Samuel 16:7; Isaiah 55:8-9). In fact, our ways are often grossly misdirected (Proverbs 14:12; Jeremiah 10:23). Therefore, we must turn to God's word in order to find outward expressions of worship acceptable to Him.

Most of you are familiar with what is commonly called the "five acts of worship." These are: singing, praying, preaching, partaking of the Lord's Supper, and giving. All of these are outward expressions of worship authorized by the New Testament. In the first century, embattled saints strove mightily to defend their right to express their worship in these ways. However, today it appears that many Christians do not even understand their true significance, neither do they stand for their right to continue to use them as authorized items of worship. The problem is that, too often, we have concentrated upon methodology without emphasizing the meaning behind these expressions. Young people are learning how to beat four-four time when they lead singing, but do they understand why they are singing? Little children are given dimes and quarters to drop in the plate as it is passed on Sunday morning, but as they grow are they taught the true significance of contributing to the Lord?

The way that we can bring meaning and a sense of privilege back to these fundamental expressions is not through adding innovations like instruments of music and dramatic performances. There is no need to leave the New Testament pattern for worship. If we read and study what the Bible says regarding these five expressions, we will find them to be profoundly meaningful!

1. *Singing.* Paul wrote, "Addressing one another in psalms and hymns and spiritual songs, singing and making melody to the Lord with all your heart" (Ephesians 5:19). Additionally, to the Colossians he wrote, "Let the word of Christ dwell in you richly, teaching and admonishing one another in all wisdom, singing psalms and hymns and spiritual songs, with thankfulness in your hearts to God" (3:16). The emphasis in popular religion has been put upon the *music* or *sound* of psalms and hymns and spiritual songs. This is because that's what appeals to us. But God never asked us to give Him orchestral arrangements, pipe organs, or rock and roll music. Paul put the emphasis upon the *words* of these songs. We are to use them to "address," "teach," and "admonish"

one another. There is no mention of audible melodies which soothe the ears, but rather inward, thankful melodies of the heart. When Paul wrote of the music of the church, he wrote of meaningful music, music that teaches and inspires.

Before someone adds to the New Testament pattern of worship by introducing instruments of music, he ought to ask, "Whom am I trying to impress?" In both of the verses cited above, Paul made reference to the fact that we are to sing "to the Lord" or "to God." Therefore, we should appeal to Him as we sing. If God had wanted Christians to use instruments, He would have prescribed their use through Christ and the apostles. After all, the strains of trumpets, harps, tambourines, and stringed instruments were commonly heard in Jewish worship (Psalm 150). They could have easily been adapted to the assemblies of the church. But God, for some reason, chose to eliminate them.

2. *Praying*. Jesus warned that, if we are not careful, our own religion could rob our prayers of meaning! The religion of the Pharisees ruined their prayers, because it emphasized being seen (Matthew 6:5-6). Likewise, pagan religion ruined prayer in that it emphasized length and repetition (Matthew 6:7-8). Because of its frequent use, in many churches today prayer has become a meaningless rite and has lost its true significance.

Go back to the New Testament, and you will learn the meaning of prayer. Jesus taught us to "Ask...seek...and knock" in order to petition our heavenly Father who gives good things to those who ask him (Matthew 7:7-9). He also said, "And whatever you ask in prayer, you will receive, if you have faith" (Matthew 21:22). Paul said, "Do not be anxious about anything, but in everything by prayer and supplication with thanksgiving let your requests be made known to God. And the peace of God, which surpasses all understanding, will guard your hearts and your minds in

Christ Jesus" (Philippians 4:6-7). Furthermore, it is explained that we can draw near with confidence to the "throne of grace, that we may receive mercy and find grace to help in time of need" (Hebrews 4:16).

3. *Preaching.* Preaching is falling on hard times these days. Some are saying that it is "outdated" and "irrelevant." It is true that, in a culture adapted to fast food and television, it can be difficult to get people to sit still long enough to listen to a gospel sermon.

However, preaching is the means by which God authorized the communication of the gospel, which is His "power for salvation to everyone who believes" (Romans 1:16). The word "power" is derived from the same word responsible for the English word "dynamite." Obviously God considers preaching to be meaningful.

What would happen if preachers just gave up and stopped preaching? Who would share the gospel with others? How would anybody know how to be saved? How would they know of the dangers of sin or of the atoning power of the blood of Christ? How would they learn of heaven or hell?

> For everyone who calls on the name of the Lord will be saved. But how are they to call on him in whom they have not believed? And how are they to believe in him of whom they have never heard? And how are they to hear without someone preaching? …How beautiful are the feet of those who preach the good news! (Romans 10:13-15).

4. *The Lord's Supper.* Jesus put meaning into the Lord's Supper when He distributed the unleavened bread and the fruit of the vine among His disciples and said, "Do this in remembrance of me" (1 Corinthians 11:24). In Paul's words, "For as often as you eat this bread and drink the cup, you proclaim the Lord's death until he comes" (1 Corinthians 11:26). How could anyone take

this memorial feast lightly? A flippant attitude towards something so important will certainly bring about severe penalties! (1 Corinthians 11:27-29).

The following suggestions will help you treat this Supper as the memorial it was meant to be:
- Read key passages on the Lord's death, like Psalm 22, Isaiah 53, and the gospel accounts of the crucifixion.
- Concentrate on the words of an appropriate song.
- Contemplate the physical, emotional, and spiritual suffering that occurred on the cross.
- Meditate upon some specific blessing for which the Lord's death is responsible (e.g., redemption, fellowship and unity, heaven, etc.).

5. *Giving.* Too often, the contribution is simply viewed as a means for meeting the budget proposed by the elders. This is a mistake. For one thing, this attitude allows disagreement with the elders to become an excuse for giving less. Someone might say, "I don't think we ought to be putting so much emphasis on mission work in Africa, so I'm holding back my contribution to let the elders know I disagree with them." A person who treats giving this lightly does not even view it as worship, but as a mere fund-raising scheme.

Paul saw that giving possessed spiritual import. For example, when he encouraged the Corinthians to contribute to the collection for the poor saints in Judea, he explained, "For the ministry of this service is not only supplying the needs of the saints, but is also overflowing in many thanksgivings to God" (2 Corinthians 9:12). Commenting on the generosity of the Philippians, he said, "I am well supplied, having received from Epaphroditus the gifts you sent, a fragrant offering, a sacrifice acceptable and pleasing to God" (Philippians 4:18). In both cases money contributed to some physical need, but Paul called it worship to God! For this reason, we should never give just to support the budget, although it is necessary that we do so. However, our first priority ought to be to bring an offering to the Lord.

There is nothing empty or ritualistic about the five expressions of worship revealed in the New Testament. All of them are packed with meaning. Through these acts, we may express true worship from the heart. This is a privilege we ought to appreciate. This is a privilege for which we must stand!

Exercises

Fill In The Blanks
1. Abraham named a mountain in Moriah _____.
2. The Jews in Malachi's day said of worship, "What _____ is this!"
3. If we want worship to be meaningful, we have to get back to the _____ of the Bible.
4. The most common word used for worship in the New Testament literally means to _____ _____.
5. "God is _____, and those who worship him must worship in _____ and _____" (John 4:24).
6. "Panting" means one should have a spiritual _____ that leads him to worship.
7. The proper end of worship is _____.
8. _____ dominates the assembly halls of popular religion.
9. Although worship begins internally, it must be expressed _____.
10. There are five expressions of worship: _____, _____, _____, _____, _____.

Discussion
1. Why do some people think worship services are boring? Are any of their reasons legitimate? What can be done by the leaders of a congregation to improve worship? What can be done by the individual worshipper to improve worship?
2. Consider the five expressions of worship. Discuss the meaning behind each of them. Do you consider them to be privileges?

8
Stand For Modesty

In Luke 8:26-36, we read of an interesting event that occurred in the "country of the Gerasenes, which is opposite Galilee." Here, Jesus and His disciples encountered a poor man whom Luke portrays in the following manner:

> For a long time he had worn no clothes, and he had not lived in a house but among the tombs...For many a time it [the unclean spirit] had seized him. He was kept under guard and bound with chains and shackles, but he would break the bonds and be driven by the demon into the desert.

There were so many demons in this man, that when Jesus asked their name, they replied, "Legion." Their very name implied that they numbered into the thousands. Having compassion on the man, the Lord cast them out, and upon losing their human host, they entered a large herd of pigs. Subsequently, the herd rushed down a steep bank into a lake and was drowned.

When reports of this amazing incident reached the ears of the people of that region, they all came out to see the man who was formerly possessed by Legion. When they arrived on the scene, they were astonished to find him "sitting at the feet of Jesus, *clothed and in his right mind.*"

The point Luke had in mind was the awesome power of the Lord over the dark forces, but I want to capitalize on that little epithet he used to describe the man Jesus helped: "clothed and in his right mind." Would that be a good description of you? Today, we don't have trouble with demon possession, but we could use more people who are "clothed and in their right mind." If some of our young people were living in Jesus' day, the citizens of the Gerasenes might be convinced that Legion had paid a visit to them also!

Our society certainly doesn't encourage us to dress modestly. Over the last fifty years, fashion has continued to cut clothing until there is almost nothing left! Sex crimes and harassment pepper our newspapers on a daily basis. Much of this is due to a disregard—by men and women—for modesty.

Can a Christian young person be "clothed and in his right mind" and still maintain an active social life among his peers? Of course he can! In fact, it is my conviction that the biblical standards of modesty promote a healthier outlook on things like human sexuality, self-esteem, and influence.

The Importance of this Subject

Generally speaking, "modesty" refers to that which is moderate or proper. With regard to clothing, the word is found only one time in the New Testament: "Likewise, I want women to adorn themselves with proper clothing, modestly and discreetly..." (1 Timothy 2:9, NASB). Interestingly, the word translated "modestly" is related to the word commonly translated "world." Both of these words are rooted in the idea of order and arrangement. Thus, biblical modesty concerns clothing that is "orderly, well-arranged, decent, modest."[14]

Actually, biblical modesty involves more than well-arranged clothing. It also includes a good balance between outer and inner beauty, a point that is supported by the rest of Paul's instruction on modesty in 1 Timothy 2:

Likewise, I want women to adorn themselves with proper clothing, modestly and discreetly, not with braided hair and gold or pearls or costly garments, but rather by means of good works, as befits women making a claim to godliness (vv. 9-10; cf. 1 Peter 3:3-4).

Usually, when the subject of modesty is discussed, several different issues are involved:
- *Revealing clothing* like swimsuits, short-shorts, and clothes that are too tight or that expose too much skin (cf. Exodus 28:42).
- *"Gender-bender" styles.* These are clothes, jewelry, and styles that hide a man's masculinity or a woman's femininity (cf. Deuteronomy 22:5).
- *The question of formal vs. informal.* Sometimes the modesty of an outfit is determined by the setting in which it is worn. You would not wear a baseball uniform to a funeral, and hopefully you would not consider wearing a tuxedo to go fishing.

One could spend hours discussing how long shorts must be or what is too tight. But, for the most part, these are matters of common sense. The true importance of the subject of modesty hangs upon one truth: *Your clothing makes a statement*. Actually, it makes two statements: (1) It says something about *who you are*; and (2) it says something *to others around you*.

For example, when Adam and Eve were first created, the Bible says, "And the man and his wife were both naked and were not ashamed" (Genesis 2:25). However, after they sinned, they made clothes of fig leaves. Those leaves made a statement. They exposed a change that had come over Adam and Eve. The mother and father of the human race were no longer innocent; they were ashamed.

Usually, the statement clothing makes depends upon

culture. For instance, when Rebekah lifted up her eyes and saw her future husband Isaac, "she took her veil and covered herself" (Genesis 24:65). Back then, her response was a sign of respect and purity. In America today it would mean nothing. In Leviticus 19:27-28, Moses writes the following rule, "You shall not round off the hair on your temples or mar the edges of your beard. You shall not make any cuts on your body for the dead or tattoo yourselves: I am the Lord." In Moses' day, those hairstyles and tattoos marked idol worshippers. So the Lord forbade the Israelites to look that way. Today, however, no such connotation would be derived. In 1 Corinthians 11:5, Paul writes, "Every wife who prays or prophesies with her head uncovered [i.e., without a veil] dishonors her head...." In the city of Paul's readers, the prostitutes identified themselves by appearing in public not wearing a veil. If a Christian woman in Corinth appeared in public in this manner, she would be identified as a prostitute and would bring reproach on the church. Thus, guidelines regarding dress were necessary so that the right statement would be made. These three examples from the Bible show that culture often regulates the statements that are made by our clothing.

Modesty's Effects On You

Your apparel says something *about who you are*. In other words, modesty can have a positive impact upon you. Let's examine the truthfulness of that statement in more detail.

1. *Modesty will instill and maintain in you a sense of shame.* When Mark Twain said that humans are the only animals that blush, or need to, he did not anticipate that there would be a movement to extinguish embarrassment from the human psyche. The clothing that many people are wearing today would bring upon them the same condemnation issued in Jeremiah's day:

Were they ashamed when they committed abomination? No, they were not at all ashamed; they did not know how to blush. Therefore they shall fall among those who fall; at the time that I punish them, they shall be overthrown... (Jeremiah 6:15).

What our society needs today is a little more old fashioned embarrassment and shame.

I realize that this may sound odd. We don't like to be embarrassed. Even the posture assumed upon being ashamed—the covered eyes, the blush-red face, the running and hiding—indicates that embarrassment introduces an uncomfortable moment. But have you ever stopped to consider that God put shame in us for a reason? Embarrassment is not some immature trait to overcome. It is something quite valuable that far too many have lost. Shame protects us. It warns us of danger ahead and tells us when to run. When young ladies are ashamed, they are not treated as property—something to be used and then thrown away. When young men are ashamed, they learn respect, and they receive it in return. In fact, modesty coupled with a sense of shame is more attractive than promiscuity ever was. Anybody can show skin. But truly interesting people have personalities that attract, and they don't have to depend on their bodies to get people to notice them.

Notice that in the King James Version, Paul's wording in 1 Timothy 2:9 is rendered "...in modest apparel, with *shamefacedness* and sobriety." Shame is an inseparable part of modesty.

2. *Modesty will promote a sense of self-worth*. The value of a healthy self-esteem has already been discussed in this book. Usually, when a young person squeezes into a tight dress or wears an outlandish hairstyle, he or she is suffering from a low self-esteem.

Some young person may object, saying, "I am expressing my independence!" But in reality, those attention-seeking clothes have been borrowed from MTV, rock and roll, and magazines. They are a reflection of the exact opposite of independence—deep insecurity and dependence upon the standards set by those who are "popular."

A person who dresses modestly has confidence in himself. She doesn't need the consent of the fashion world. She has the boldness to express independence, like Lillian Hellman who said, "I cannot and will not cut my conscience to fit this year's fashion." By dressing modestly, she is saying, "I am important enough to be noticed for something other than my clothes." Queen Vashti expressed that strong sense of self-worth when she refused to be paraded before her drunk husband and his guests (Esther 1:11-12). She knew she was more than a piece of meat, and she demanded to be treated with respect.

3. *Modesty will direct you toward your highest calling: the glorification of God*. A Christian's duty is not to win a popularity contest or to be listed as "most attractive" in the school yearbook. A Christian's duty is to attract attention to the Father using every available means (Matthew 5:16; 1 Corinthians 6:20). Those who struggle with immodesty need to answer a question: When you wear too little or too much, who is getting the attention?

This is Peter's point in his instruction to Christian wives:

> Do not let your adorning be external—the braiding of hair, the wearing of gold, or the putting on of clothing—but let your adorning be the hidden person of the heart with the imperishable beauty of a gentle and quiet spirit, which in God's sight is very precious (1 Peter 3:3-4).

They were not to attract attention to themselves by external "adorning." Rather they were to adorn themselves with character, "the hidden person of the heart." This clothing has an "imperishable beauty" and is "very precious" in God's sight.

Modesty's Effects On Others

Not only does modesty say something *about who you are*, but it also says something *to those around you*. Frequently, when parents forbid things like mixed swimming or immodest clothing, a young person will protest, saying, "I can't help it if they look at me that way. They shouldn't lust! It's not my fault if they struggle with temptation!" Part of that is true. One should avoid any lust that will lead him to sin (Matthew 5:28; 2 Timothy 2:22; James 1:13-15). However, it is wrong to argue that we are not somewhat responsible when other people lust because of the way we dress. Modesty, or a lack thereof, has an effect upon others.

Jesus said, "Temptations to sin are sure to come, but woe to the one through whom they come! It would be better for him if a millstone were hung around his neck and he were cast into the sea than that he should cause one of these little ones to sin" (Luke 17:1-2). A millstone is an enormous boulder. It is hard to imagine a circumstance worse than having one of those things tied around your neck and being tossed into the sea. Christ, however, could imagine such a circumstance. He said that causing someone to stumble is worse. Thus, anytime our dress or appearance makes a negative impact upon another's spiritual condition, we are putting ourselves in a precarious situation.

Appearance doesn't only have a negative impact upon others. When one dresses modestly, he can become a powerful influence for good. When Queen Vashti refused the command of her irresponsible husband, all the men grew worried, saying, "For the queen's behavior will be made known to all women, causing them to look at their husbands with contempt..." (Esther 1:17). In other words, they were afraid that, through the queen's influence, they would no longer be able to treat their wives like property. If that influence continued, women might start commanding respect! Oh that we would have more young people who were willing to take a stand like Vashti! With that kind of influence, we could change the world!

What you wear speaks volumes about who you are and what you want to say to others. Beauty is only skin deep, but modesty is buried much deeper. Modesty is important, so when it comes to your appearance, don't cave to society's advice. Make your stand!

Exercises

Fill In The Blanks
1. After Jesus was through with the man possessed by Legion, he was _____ and in his _____ mind.
2. Biblical modesty concerns clothing that is _____, well-arranged, _____, and modest.
3. Modest includes a good _____ between outer and inner beauty.
4. Your clothing says something about _____ you are.
5. Your clothing says something to _____ around you.
6. Usually, the statement clothing makes depends upon _____.
7. Modesty will instill in you a sense of _____.
8. Modesty will promote a sense of self _____.
9. The Christian's highest calling is the _____ of _____.
10. It is better to have a _____ tied to your neck and be tossed into the sea than to cause someone to _____.

Discussion
1. What are some of the "gender-blender" styles that young people are wearing today? Do these really affect a person's Christian influence?
2. Name some clothing trends that have made statements—good and bad.
3. What are the benefits of shame?

9 Stand Against Satan

So far we have been on the offensive. A Christian must fight *for* a number of things, and with that in mind, we have studied a number of offensive efforts:
- Stand for Your Faith
- Stand for Yourself
- Stand for God's Word
- Stand for the Worship Privileges
- Stand for Modesty

In this battle you must also go on the defensive, for you must stand *against* a number of things. This will be our concentration for the rest of this study.

In Ephesians 6:10-20, the apostle Paul commands his readers to "put on the whole armor of God." This spiritual armor is comprised of several parts: the "belt of truth," the "breastplate of righteousness," "shoes" which symbolize "the readiness given by the gospel of peace," the "shield of faith," the "helmet of salvation," and the "sword of the Spirit" which is the word of God. All of this battle gear is directly related to our study. Paul says, "Therefore take up the whole armor of God, that you may be able to withstand in the evil day, and having done all, to *stand firm. Stand therefore...*" (vv. 13-14).

Why exactly are we to wear all of this protective gear in making our stand? Whom are we to stand against? Look carefully at verse 11: "Put on the whole armor of God, that you may be able to stand against the schemes of the devil." The devil is our enemy. It is important that we learn how to stand against him.

Paul says that the devil has "schemes." This word is translated from a Greek term that sounds like our English word "method." The word is plural. The apostle is warning us that Satan has several methods in his arsenal to bring about the ruin of our souls. In another passage, Paul calls them "designs" (2 Corinthians 2:11). If we are going to wage war successfully with an enemy who has "schemes," we are going to need to learn his clever ways, or we will be defeated. Consider just four methods the devil uses against us.

Method #1: He Comforts

According to a survey conducted by the Barna Research Group, not many people actually believe that Satan is a real person. It was reported that 43 percent of those who claim to be "born again" Christians said they believed Satan was only a symbol of evil and not an actual being. Another five percent said they didn't know for sure whether he was real or not. Therefore, almost half of professing Christians doubt the devil is a real person who is seeking to destroy them. Satan smiles at statistics like this. They prove that half of so-called Christian worshippers are right where he wants them. They are comfortable and unguarded—they don't even think he exists. This works perfectly into his plan. He likes the ambush, the surprise attack.

The idea of an ambush is inherent in the word we earlier applied to the devil's opposition: "schemes." The King James Version uses the word "wiles." The language conveys the idea of methods that are cunning and deceptive. A more obtuse enemy might be quite forward in his attack, but Satan is not that obvious. He wants to see you comfortable and at ease before he ruins you.

The devil is not going to rely upon an open assault.

He may come disguised as an "angel of light" (2 Corinthians 11:14), or he may come in the form of a trusted friend (this is one of the ways he tempted Christ; see Luke 22:3). Also, he cleverly times his assaults to catch his victims off guard. He will strike when you least expect it. One has warned that the Christian must beware of the devil's "vacation" because he uses brief episodes of peace to surprise the unaware. Also, if he fails on the first attempt, be assured that he will return. At the close of Luke's account of the temptation of Jesus, he added that the devil "departed from him until an opportune time" (4:13). He is not going to wage an open, continuous assault. Instead, he will opt for the surprise attack.

Peter believed that the devil was real. He had been tricked by him. He had let his guard down and consequently had experienced a great setback (Matthew 26:33-35, 69-75). Much later, after he had overcome his sin, he warned of a real, influential presence, saying, "Be sober-minded; be watchful. Your adversary the devil prowls around like a roaring lion, seeking someone to devour" (1 Peter 5:8). Knowing how Satan likes to pounce on those who are comfortably at ease, Peter demanded "sober-mindedness" and "watchfulness." Don't get too comfortable. It takes vigilance to stand against Satan.

Method #2: He Teaches

The devil would like to teach you his own gospel. In truth, the idea of the devil's gospel is nonsense. The word "gospel" means "good news," and there is nothing good about the devil's message. However, the Bible does speak of "different" gospels (2 Corinthians 11:4; Galatians 1:7-10), that is, gospels other than the true "teaching of Christ" (2 John 9-11). In every case, these opposing gospels are categorically condemned. Anyone who subscribes to them is said to be "accursed." Certainly this would be the fate of the individual who adheres to the devil's gospel.

When the devil teaches, it is important to remember that he is "a liar and the father of lies" (John 8:44). Nothing he says can be trusted. Yet people are gathering in droves to sit at his feet. What are some of the doctrines that comprise the devil's gospel?

1. "How you feel matters more than what you know." Every day, millions of people make decisions largely based on their emotions. A person may decide to take a job, buy a car, or decide to go to college because of the way he feels. Is there anything wrong with being guided by emotions?

Sometimes emotions are helpful. In fact, the human experience is enhanced by the capacity to feel. But can we allow our emotions to be our sole guide in making important decisions? Should we choose a marriage partner on raw emotions? What about religion? Can we let our sentimentality be our guide? The devil would like us to think so.

Satan wants us to live by our emotions because they will many times lead us astray. Most sins are driven by emotion. Murder is driven by rage. Adultery is caused by passion. Business malpractice is motivated by greed. If our feelings can lead us down such awful paths, can we really trust them?

Another problem with emotions is that they are always grounded in human thought, which has a poor track record in matters pertaining to spirituality (Proverbs 14:12; Jeremiah 10:23). Remember Naaman? He felt that the waters of the Jordan River were too dirty to heal him of his leprosy, but he was not cleansed until he heeded the command of a prophet of God (2 Kings 5:1-14). The devil wants you to listen to emotions, but only God's word can sufficiently guide you in matters of significance (2 Timothy 3:16-17; 2 Peter

1:3).

2. "Popularity is the greatest achievement." Nobody reading this would admit that this teaching is true, and yet many young people live as if it were factual. The devil knows that human beings desire companionship (cf. Genesis 2:18; Proverbs 17:17; 27:9), so he takes advantage of that need and tries to make it the top priority in our lives.

At times, we must risk loneliness in order to remain faithful to God. Jesus Himself dealt with this challenge; He knows what loneliness is like (John 6:66; Matthew 26:56). Like Him, we must learn to lean on the Father in times of loneliness (John 16:32). Also, let's not forget that we are never without companions in the church. There are "seven thousand that have not bowed to Baal" (1 Kings 19:18).

3. "God's laws may be disobeyed without suffering any consequences." With this doctrine, Satan convinces his followers to procrastinate obedience until it is too late. This is his oldest teaching on record. He uttered it through the serpent's lips in Eden, saying, "You will not surely die" (Genesis 3:4), and he continues to speak it even today. Don't believe his lies. Those who die outside of Christ will suffer eternal punishment. The Bible makes this point very plain (Romans 2:4-11; 2 Thessalonians 1:7-9; Revelation 20:11-15; 21:8).

Method #3: He Sifts

Next to Jesus Christ, Satan coveted Simon Peter more than anyone else. And at one point, he almost had the apostle. Peter had stooped to denying the Master he once swore to protect (Matthew 26:69-75). Jesus had warned him of this in an intriguing passage recorded by Luke:

Simon, Simon, behold, Satan demanded to have

you, that he might sift you like wheat, but I have prayed for you that your faith may not fail. And when you have turned again, strengthen your brothers (22:31-32).

What did Jesus mean when He said that Satan wanted to "sift" Peter like wheat?

When wheat is harvested from the fields, it is composed of two basic parts: the grain, the inner part later used for food, and the chaff, the useless husk covering the grain. During Jesus' days, a two-part process was used to separate the grain from the chaff. First, the wheat was beaten. This would break the grain loose from the chaff. Then the wheat was "sifted." This process involved tossing or agitating the wheat with a winnowing fan. The end result was that the grain would remain in the fan, and the chaff would be thrown off. Jesus was telling Peter that Satan wanted to "sift" him in his winnowing fan. That is, he wanted to shake or agitate Peter in order to see whether any of his faith would remain, or whether all of it would be found to be useless "chaff" (e.g., emotional ties, trend following, etc.). In other words, Jesus was telling Peter that his faith was about to be tested. That is why the Lord said, "I have prayed for you that your *faith* may not fail."

Be assured that Satan wants to sift you too. He will try to shake you up with anything he can: peer pressure, hardship, persecution, ridicule, evil desire, greed, lies, etc. But you can also be certain that Christ is praying for you that your faith may not fail. Peter was sifted, but he overcame in the end. You can defeat the devil too.

Method #4: He Tempts

The devil has worn many names. Throughout scripture, we see him called "serpent" (Genesis 3:4), "Satan" (Matthew 4:10), "Beelzebub" and the "Prince of

Demons" (Matthew 12:24), the "Ruler of this World" (John 14:30), the "God of this World" (2 Corinthians 4:4), "Belial" (2 Corinthians 6:15), the "Prince of the Power of the Air" (Ephesians 2:2), the "Ruler of Darkness" (Ephesians 6:12), the "Angel of the Bottomless Pit," "Abaddon," "Apollyon" (Revelation 9:11), and "Accuser" (Revelation 12:10).

There is one last name that is particularly fitting: the name "Tempter" (Matthew 4:3). James makes it clear that God tempts no one (1:13). The devil, on the other hand, has made temptation his specialty. Only he would be so brazen as to tempt the Son of God! If he will go to great lengths to drive Jesus to sin, certainly he will try to tempt you.

Too many of us fail to prepare for temptation. We are like the little boy who was told by his father not to swim in the canal. A few hours later, he walked back into the house toting a wet pair of swimming trunks. "Where have you been?" his father asked angrily. The boy replied, "Swimming in the canal." Astonished, the father said, "I thought I told you not to swim in that canal. Why did you do it?" "Because," said the boy, "I had my swimming trunks with me, and I just couldn't resist the temptation to swim." Trying to be patient, the father asked, "Why did you carry your swimming trunks with you when I had already told you not to go swimming?" To this the young man replied, "Well, I carried them with me just in case I was tempted to swim!" Don't be like that little boy. Instead, be determined to defeat temptation.

One thing you can do to prepare for temptation is learn how it works. Temptation is a lot like a trap used to catch wild animals. It depends on two things: hunger and bait. If a trapper has bait, but the animals aren't hungry, he is not likely to catch anything. Likewise, if the animals are hungry, but he forgot to bring the bait, he is going home empty-handed. This may have been the principle James had in mind when he wrote,

> But each person is tempted when he is lured and enticed by his own desire. Then desire when it has conceived gives birth to sin, and sin when it is fully grown brings forth death (1:14-15).

According to James, there are two steps to being tempted. First, a person must be "lured." The Greek behind the word here is related to the idea of "bait." So temptation involves being lured by some kind of "bait." In a scenario where temptation takes place, the bait is simply an opportunity to sin. Secondly, James says that a person must be "enticed by his own desire." This is the "hunger" we were talking about. Sometimes it is called "lust." This enticement is the desire within a person that makes him want to commit the sin.

Remember the two steps that make up temptation, and you can avoid it. If you can guard your heart against unwholesome desires, then you won't hunger for sin. Jesus said, "Blessed are those who hunger and thirst for righteousness, for they shall be satisfied" (Matthew 5:6). "Righteousness," then, ought to be the object of every Christian's desire. Furthermore, if you can avoid those places where "bait" might lure you into sin, you may be able to stay away from temptation. For instance, if you are trying to maintain your purity, don't get into tempting situations with members of the opposite sex. Try to stay in public, or go on double dates. If you want to abstain from drinking alcohol, avoid parties where people are drinking. Many times, temptation can be averted simply by avoiding the "bait" (Proverbs 4:14-15; Ephesians 4:27).

Another thing that one can do to defeat the devil's tempting schemes is to look for the escape route. God promised that, when you are tempted, there will always be a way of escape (1 Corinthians 10:13). That does not mean that escaping sin will always be easy or that you will be immediately rewarded. Joseph was imprisoned when he fled the seduction of Potiphar's wife (Genesis 39). But, like Joseph, you will be rewarded in the end when you resist the devil (James 4:7).

Finally, an active prayer life can prepare you to fight temptation. In the "Model Prayer," Jesus taught us to pray, "And lead us not into temptation, but deliver us from evil" (Matthew 6:13). Also, when Peter, James, and John accompanied Jesus to the Garden of Gethsemane, He told them, "Watch and pray that you may not enter into temptation. The spirit indeed is willing, but the flesh is weak" (Matthew 26:41). In the public services of the church, the men often pray looking backward on the sins already committed, saying, "Father, forgive us for our sins," but how many times do we pray, "Father, lead us not into temptation, but deliver us from evil?" We need to start praying that we may avoid sin altogether. Then we can pray the prayer for forgiveness less frequently.

We must stand against the devil. But we can only do this if we learn of his schemes. Study these things, and wear your Christian armor. Do everything you must do to stand!

Exercises

Fill In The Blanks
1. Paul commands us to put on the whole _____ of God.
2. We must beware of the devil's _____.
3. Satan can disguise himself as an _____ of light.
4. The devil departed from Christ until an _____ time.
5. Satan prefers a _____ attack.
6. Peter compared the devil to a _____ _____.
7. The devil wants you to listen to your _____, but only God's _____ can be your true guide.
8. Satan told Eve, "You shall not surely _____."
9. The devil wanted to _____ Peter like wheat.
10. Temptation is a lot like a _____ used to catch wild animals.
11. When you are tempted, you should look for an _____ route.
12. An active _____ _____ can prepare you to fight temptation.

Discussion
1. Do you believe the devil is real? What are some evidences of his existence?
2. Have your friends ever been motivated to do something pertaining to religion because they "felt" a certain way? Give some examples. Is emotion a safe guide in these matters?
3. Can you name some other examples of doctrines that comprise the devil's gospel?
4. Is temptation itself a sin? See Hebrews 4:15.
5. What are some exceptionally strong temptations for teenagers? How can these be defeated?

10
Stand Against God's Enemies

Three kingdoms had come to do battle with Jehoshaphat and the people of God. The Moabites, the Ammonites, and the inhabitants of Mount Seir were quickly approaching Jerusalem from the south. Something had to be done. So Jehoshaphat, king of Judah, assembled his people together in the house of the Lord and petitioned the God of heaven:

> ...Behold, the men of Ammon and Moab and Mount Seir...reward us by coming to drive us out of your possession, which you have given us to inherit. O our God, will you not execute judgment on them? For we are powerless against this great horde that is coming against us. We do not know what to do, but our eyes are on you (2 Chronicles 20:10-12).

Jehoshaphat's prayer reached the ears of the Lord, and He answered the king through a prophet named Jahaziel,

> Do not be afraid and do not be dismayed at this great horde, for the battle is not yours but God's...Stand firm, hold your position, and see the salvation of the Lord on your behalf, O Judah and Jerusalem. Do not be afraid and do not be dismayed. Tomorrow go out against them, and the Lord will be with you (2 Chronicles 20:15, 17).

These divine words gave the people courage, and they readied themselves for the next day.

The following morning, when they visited the place to which God had instructed them to go, they found that the Lord had created confusion between the men of Ammon, Moab, and Mount Seir. Apparently there had been some disagreement, and the three kingdoms destroyed themselves! Judah did not even have to enter the battle (2 Chronicles 20:22-23). The Lord had told them, "for the battle is not yours but God's." As long as they stood firm and held their position, He would protect them from the enemy.

There is a lesson for all of us in that story. We must not be afraid to stand firm against the enemy. Ultimately, he will not succeed. All of God's enemies will fall (2 Kings 6:16; Psalm 118:6; Romans 8:31; 1 John 4:4).

The Hate of God

John gave us an important fact about the nature of God when he said, "God is love" (1 John 4:8). However, we ought not look at that statement as if it were a complete description. If love was all there was to God, He would not be omnipotent, wise, righteous, or unchanging. He would simply be "love."

Also, if love is all there is to God, He would not have the capacity to hate. It may be difficult to imagine even an ounce of hate in the personality of God, but Solomon says, "There are six things that the Lord hates, seven that are an abomination to him" (Proverbs 6:16). The list that follows is not intended to be exhaustive, for the Bible reveals several other objects of divine hatred (Leviticus 18:20-23; Deuteronomy 7:25; 18:10-11; 24:4; Proverbs 11:1; Malachi 2:16; Luke 16:15).

Please don't misunderstand. There is no hint of

malice or hostility in the nature of God. His hatred is different from man's. When the Bible says that God "hates" something, it means that He strongly dislikes things opposed to holiness and goodness. For this reason, there is not any evidence that God has ever hated people. As it is often said, "He hates sin but not the sinner."

If it is true that God hates, then it follows that He has enemies. Hate drives a person to one side or another. And whenever you take sides, you create enemies. A person's enemies are basically people who practice the things he hates. That is why sinners are referred to as God's enemies (Romans 5:10). By performing the things he hates, they place themselves on a battlefield of opposition against righteousness.

God wants you to stand firm against His enemies. There is no need to fear. "For the battle is not yours but God's." As long as we hold our position alongside the ranks of God's people, the enemy will fall before us.

God's Enemies

Let's discuss some of the enemies of God teenagers frequently face. Space will only allow us to discuss a few of the more formidable opponents threatening Christian young people.

Atheism

David said, "The fool says in his heart, 'There is no God'" (Psalm 14:1). Nobody in his right mind would look at the numerous evidences for God's existence and conclude in his head, "There is no God" (see chapter four). That is why David said the fool says *in his heart* there is no God. The position of the atheist is not rational; it is an angry and rash outburst against a living God.

Evolution is one of many unfortunate things that has trickled down from atheistic philosophy. Purportedly backed by science, this notion claims that all life originated through naturalistic processes. In other words, a few amino acids and proteins bumped around in nothingness for billions of years until *bang*, life began. The question still unanswered by evolutionists is, how did those first particles come to be? It is unlikely they will ever respond. Nothing comes from nothing, and the only explanation for an existing universe is an infinite, all-powerful God.

Although many school teachers and college professors teach evolution as fact, we must remember that it is only a theory, a proposition that has yet to be fully tested. Other theories for the origin of life exist, and some even include an Intelligent Designer, but the atheists are prevailing. They are doing everything they can to keep God out of the classroom and out of the minds of young people.

Atheism has made a devastating impact on society. In particular, it has changed the way people value human life. Horrific practices like abortion and euthanasia are just two of the many awful things devised by minds that deny the existence of God. Christians must prepare to defend their faith against atheism and do everything possible to squelch its powerful influence.

Sexual Immorality

Sex is not evil. It was created by God for the enjoyment of mankind and the propagation of the human race. But God has set boundaries for sexual relationships. According to His word, this special bond is reserved only for a man and a woman in a marriage relationship (Proverbs 5:15-20; Hebrews 13:4).

Society is challenging this divine instruction from all

sides. The entertainment industry mocks it. In political circles it is challenged. Educational establishments scorn it. This presents a great challenge for all Christians, but for young people in particular. However, we must stand against sexual immorality. It is an enemy of God.

God opposes those who ignore the proper *contract* for a sexual relationship. Marriage was designed by God to be the only place for sexual fulfillment. This bond is not a human institution. It is a lifelong contract made between a husband, a wife, and God (Matthew 19:4-9). Whenever two people ignore that contract and change God's guidelines for sexual relationships (such as premarital sex, adultery, fornication), they put themselves in a precarious spiritual condition (1 Corinthians 6:9-11; Galatians 5:19-21).

God also opposes those who ignore the proper *orientation* for a sexual relationship. This is a point the apostle Paul argued forcefully in his letter to the church at Rome:

> For this reason God gave them up to dishonorable passions. For their women exchanged natural relations for those that are contrary to nature; and the men likewise gave up natural relations with women and were consumed with passion for one another, men committing shameless acts with men and receiving in themselves the due penalty for their error (1:26-27).

Homosexuality is a sin. It is true that some are raised in families or environments that condition them to adopt a sexual orientation other than the one endorsed by God in His word. However, a homosexual is not excused by these circumstances any more than an adulterer or a thief is excused by past circumstances that may have conditioned his behavior. God calls on all who are involved in "alternate lifestyles" to leave their sinful practices and stand for what is right. "God will judge the sexually immoral and adulterous" (Hebrews 13:4).

Sins of the Tongue

In the wisdom literature of the Old Testament, we read, "The mouth of the righteous is a fountain of life, but the mouth of the wicked conceals violence" (Proverbs 10:11). Again, it says, "Death and life are in the power of the tongue..." (Proverbs 18:21). Both of these verses were constructed to enforce this point: The tongue is a powerful instrument of the human body. It can be used for good, or it can be used for evil (cf. James 3:1-12).

Young people frequently struggle with their speech. In fact, it is not uncommon for a young person to become an enemy of God just by the way that he talks. Consider some of the following forms of speech condemned in the scriptures:
- Gossip and slander (Proverbs 10:18; 17:4; 20:19; 26:20).
- Lying (Proverbs 6:16-19; Revelation 21:8).
- Boasting (Proverbs 8:13; 14:3; 26:12; 27:1).
- Profanity or foul language (Matthew 12:36; Ephesians 5:4; James 3:9-10).
- Evil speaking (Proverbs 24:1-2; Ephesians 4:31; 5:4).
- Flattery or hypocritical praise (Proverbs 6:24; 20:19; 29:5).

Division

The measure of God's love of unity (Psalm 133) is equal to His hate for division. In Proverbs 6:16-19, Solomon writes of "six things that the Lord hates, seven that are an abomination to him." Some scholars believe that this figure of speech (i.e., "six things...seven") introduces a climactic progression. In other words, the list begins with the least of the abominations and ends with the worst. If that is the case, then the sin at the bottom of the list is exceedingly despised by God. And do you know what made item number seven? "One who sows discord among brothers." There is no doubt that God hates division among His people.

The church at Corinth struggled with division. Evidently, there was no little disagreement over who was the best preacher. Some were saying, "I follow Paul," or "I follow Apollos," or "I follow Cephas," and somehow a wedge had been driven between the members of that congregation. Paul called them "infants" (1 Corinthians 3:1) and rebuked them, saying, "I appeal to you brothers, by the name of our Lord Jesus Christ, that all of you agree and that there be no divisions among you, but that you be united in the same mind and the same judgment" (1 Corinthians 1:10).

The apostle John also had to address the problem of division in one of his letters. An individual named Diotrephes had created quite a disturbance in some congregation. He liked to "put himself first" and did not acknowledge the authority of the leadership of the church. He was a malcontent, who refused to welcome brethren and tried to oust people from the church (3 John 9-10).

It is natural for young people to have disagreements, but sometimes things get out of hand. A Christian should never create discord. Instead he ought to be doing everything possible to build up his brothers and sisters in Christ and create peace in the church (Romans 14:19).

The enemies of God abound. We have only scratched the tip of the iceberg in this discussion. Just remember that, whenever an enemy rears his ugly head, God will help you stand firm. "The battle is not yours but God's. Stand firm, hold your position, and see the salvation of the Lord."

Exercises

Fill In The Blanks
1. All of God's enemies will _____.
2. John said, "God is _____."
3. If it is true that God hates, then it follows that He has _____.
4. "The _____ says in his _____ there is no God" (Psalm 14:1).
5. _____ has trickled down from atheistic philosophy.
6. Atheism has made a _____ impact on society.
7. The sexual relationship is reserved only for a man and a woman in a _____ relationship.
8. Homosexuality is a _____.
9. Marriage is a _____ contract made between a _____, a _____, and _____.
10. "God will _____ the sexually immoral and adulterous" (Hebrews 13:4).
11. "_____ and _____ are in the power of the tongue" (Proverbs 18:21).
12. The last item in a list of things God hates is "one who sows _____ among brothers" (Proverbs 6:19).

Discussion
1. Discuss some of the objects of divine hatred (Leviticus 18:20-23; Deuteronomy 7:25; 18:10-11; 24:4; Proverbs 6:16-19; 11:1; Malachi 2:16; Luke 16:15).
2. What is the difference between God's hatred and man's hatred?
3. "Theistic evolution" is an attempt to combine the theory of evolution with a faith in God. Can a person espouse this notion without doing damage to the creation account in Genesis?
4. What is a "denomination?" What does it have to do with division? (cf. Matthew 16:18; Ephesians 4:4-6). What can be done to build unity among Christians?

11
Stand Against Drinking

The best commercials on television are those that promote the consumption of alcohol. Beer companies produce the most peaceful commercials. In them, one can see alcoholic beverages being consumed in picturesque settings of beaches, ice-capped mountains, and green forests trimmed with waterfalls. This is ironic because actually alcohol is responsible for much of the domestic strife, child abuse, and broken homes in America. Commercials promoting alcohol frequently hint that the strongest, healthiest, and most attractive representatives of humankind are beer drinkers. In actuality, alcohol is our nation's third leading cause of death, second only to heart disease and cancer. Alcoholics are far from being physically fit! These commercials are usually very humorous. That in itself is a joke. While alcohol can stimulate laughter and amusement for a time, its lasting effects include frustration, anger, and depression.

The companies that manufacture alcoholic beverages are successfully persuading young people that drinking is a desirable pastime. According to a statistic posted on the website for Mothers Against Drunk Driving (M.A.D.D.), the most popular drink among teenagers is beer. The world hasn't been honest with young people about the dangerous effects alcohol has upon the body and soul. Fortunately, however, the Bible is honest, and its pages reveal overwhelming evidence that should convince young people to make a stand against drinking alcohol.

The Bible And Drinking

No book of the Bible addresses the problem of drinking more than Proverbs. Its wisdom tells us, "Wine is a mocker, strong drink a brawler, and whoever is led astray by it is not wise" (20:1). God knows how alcohol can loosen the tongue and clench the fist, and He summarizes its consumption as "not wise."

The poetry of Proverbs 23:29-35 vividly describes the pitiful condition of every drunk—the sorrow and strife; the blood-shot eyes; the way it first "sparkles in the cup and goes down smoothly" but then "bites like a serpent and stings like an adder;" the dizzy swagger of a sailor perched on the top of a mast. It's all there. The writer even describes the unconscious, unruly behavior of the inebriated: "'They struck me,' you will say, 'but I was not hurt; they beat me, but I did not feel it. When shall I awake?'" The passage ends with the sad statement spoken by the lips of every person hooked on booze: "I must have another drink."

According to the book of Proverbs, there is no way a man can consume alcohol and fill a position of responsibility. "It is not for kings, O Lemuel, it is not for kings to drink wine, or for rulers to take strong drink, lest they drink and forget what has been decreed and pervert the rights of all the afflicted" (31:4-5). History agrees. Noah would have had a perfect record had it not been for a night of intoxication (Genesis 9:20-23). Elah might have made a great king for Israel, but he was assassinated in the first year of his reign. How did his enemies get the upper hand? He was "drinking himself drunk in the house of Arza" (1 Kings 16:9). The Israelites struck down the armies of Ben-hadad and thirty-two other kings because they were celebrating a drunken feast in the middle of the day (1 Kings 20:16). The night that Belshazzar, king of Babylon, saw the handwriting on the wall that spelled his doom, he was drinking wine out of golden vessels stolen from the temple of God (Daniel 5).

The book of Proverbs is not alone in its prohibitions regarding strong drink. The New Testament proposes condemnations of equal weight (Luke 21:34; Galatians 5:21; 1 Timothy 3:3; 1 Peter 4:3). From cover to cover, the Bible warns its readers of the dangers of drinking.

These strong warnings are important to remember when someone argues that it is acceptable for the Christian to consume alcohol. Often one will bring up Christ's first miracle in Cana, when He turned water into wine (John 2:1-12). On this occasion Jesus and the rest of His family attended a wedding. When the wine ran out, Jesus amazed everyone by miraculously changing plain water into wine. It is argued that if Christ opposed drinking, He would not have performed a miracle that actually encouraged people to drink wine. However, at the wedding feast in Cana, Jesus produced around 180 gallons of wine! If this had been alcoholic, then the first miracle of Christ would have placed Him in direct contradiction with the Bible! Because we know that Jesus never sinned (Hebrews 4:15), we can rest assured He was not making alcoholic wine at Cana.

It is helpful to understand that "wine" is not used exclusively in the Bible to refer to intoxicating beverages. For example, in Isaiah 16:10 the prophet says, "No treader treads out wine in the presses." It doesn't take a wine expert to realize that a lengthy fermentation process must occur before alcoholic wine can reach its final stages. When it is tread in the presses, it is simply pure grape juice. Also, the idea of "new wine" necessarily refers to nonalcoholic wine. Jesus said, "Neither is new wine put into old wineskins. If it is, the skins burst and the wine is spilled and the skins are destroyed. But new wine is put into fresh wineskins, and so both are preserved" (Matthew 9:17). The prospect of putting new wine in old wineskins is dangerous because during the fermentation process, wine puts off gases that cause its container to expand. An old, brittle wineskin will burst under these circumstances, while a new one is elastic and will not. "New wine" precedes the fermentation process and is therefore nonalcoholic.

The Bible's warnings are consistent with statistics regarding the consumption of intoxicating beverages. Both reveal that drinking is dangerous to one's health and soul! Consider the following:
- Each year, college students spend approximately $5.5 billion on alcohol—more than they spend on soft drinks, milk, juice, tea, coffee, and books combined.
- About 10.1 million people age 12 to 20 years reported current use of alcohol in 2001. For 28.5 percent of this age group, alcohol is an illicit substance.
- The median age at which children begin drinking is 13. Young people who begin drinking before age 15 are four times more likely to develop alcohol dependence than those who begin drinking at age 21.
- Teenagers are not well informed about alcohol's effects. Nearly one-third of the teens responding to a 1998 American Academy of Pediatrics survey mistakenly believed that a 12-ounce can of beer contains less alcohol than a standard shot of distilled spirits.
- The total cost attributable to the consequences of underage drinking was more than $58 billion per year in 1998 dollars.
- Alcohol-related crashes in the United States cost the public more than $110 billion in 1998, including more than $40 billion in monetary costs and almost $70 billion in quality of life losses.
- More than 40 percent of individuals who start drinking before the age of 13 will develop alcohol abuse or alcohol dependence at some point in their lives.

- Alcohol affects all parts of the brain, including heart rate, coordination, speech, and destruction of brain cells.
- Heavy drinking over many years may result in serious mental disorders or permanent, irreversible damage to the brain or peripheral nervous system.
- Alcohol dilutes itself in the water volume of the body in order to travel through the system. Vital organs, like the brain, that contain a lot of water and need an ample blood supply are particularly vulnerable to the effects of alcohol.
- Fetal exposure to alcohol is a leading cause of mental retardation.
- Alcohol is a major cause of divorce, wife abuse, and child molestation.
- Alcohol is involved in 60 percent of child abuse cases, 75 percent of all broken homes, and 50 percent of all homicides.
- Alcohol is a major contributor to teen suicide attempts.
- Of 330 children born today in the U.S., one will die and one will sustain serious or crippling injuries in an alcohol-related crash before they reach the age of 24.
- In 2001, 25 percent of the young drivers 15 to 20 years old who were killed in crashes were intoxicated.
- Drunk driving is the nation's most frequently committed violent crime.[15]

What About Social Drinking?

The practice of "social drinking" involves drinking alcohol up to the point where it would impair one's judgment. Since social drinking is not responsible for drunkenness, some argue that it should be allowed.

This subject is important, for it represents a challenge frequently faced by executives, salespeople, and other professionals. Here is a common scenario: A busy executive is invited to discuss work over lunch with his boss. When the two of them take their seats at the restaurant, the boss orders a martini. He asks his employee, "Aren't you going to order a drink? I think a martini helps us to relax and improves the quality of business meetings." If the eager executive is a Christian, he is put in a difficult situation. Is it okay to have just one drink? Or will social drinking compromise his influence as a Christian?

The answer to this question for young people ought to be easy. Social drinking is illegal if you are under the age of 21, but let's discuss this subject as it pertains to those over the legal drinking age.

Those who argue in favor of social drinking usually base their case upon two misconceptions. The first is that all wine consumed during Bible times was alcoholic. As we have already proven, the Bible often refers to unfermented grape juice as "wine" (Numbers 18:12; Isaiah 16:10; Joel 2:24; Matthew 9:17). As the New Testament was being written, no Greek word existed to distinguish between alcoholic and nonalcoholic wine. Therefore, one must judge the meaning of the word "wine" in the Bible by the context in which it is used.

The second misconception used as grounds for social drinking is that drinking alcoholic beverages in the first century justifies drinking alcoholic beverages in the twenty-first century. Comparing the wine of ancient times to modern-day wine is like comparing apples with oranges. First of all, wine in those days was much weaker. Today wineries strengthen the potency of their products by mixing the pure grape juice with alcoholic substances. Secondly, when comparing our situation with that of the first century, we should take into account the fact that then wine was sometimes needed for medicinal purposes (1 Timothy 5:23). Today we have better drugs to treat our ailments effectively, all reports of wine's health benefits notwithstanding.

Thirdly, drinking water was often impure in ancient times, and there were few alternatives. Today we have an abundant supply of pure drinking water, along with a number of other nonalcoholic beverages. So even if a person finds an example of a first-century Christian's drinking, that does not justify a Christian's drinking today. Times have changed, and we do not need alcoholic beverages.

Perhaps the most important issue to consider is influence. Jesus taught that one's influence is extremely important (Luke 17:1-2). What kind of influence does a social drinker have upon a babe in Christ? Furthermore, what could happen in the mind of a converted alcoholic upon seeing a brother in Christ imbibe in intoxicating beverages? That negative influence could work irreparable damage on a new Christian!

It is best for a Christian to withdraw completely from the consumption of alcohol. This approach is endorsed by Peter, who said, "Beloved, I urge you as sojourners and exiles to *abstain* from the passions of the flesh, which wage war against your soul" (1 Peter 2:11). Take a stand against drinking alcohol. "Whoever is led astray by it is not wise" (Proverbs 20:1).

Exercises

Fill In The Blanks
1. The most popular drink among teenagers is _____.
2. "Wine is a _____, strong drink a _____, and whoever is led astray by it is not _____" (Proverbs 20:1).
3. According to Proverbs, there is no way a man can consume alcohol and fill a position of _____.
4. Christ produced around _____ gallons of wine at the wedding feast in Cana.
5. "Wine" is not used exclusively in the Bible to refer to _____ _____.
6. Alcohol-related crashes in the U.S. cost the public more than _____ in 1998.
7. Alcohol affects _____ parts of the brain.
8. Heavy drinking over many years may result in serious _____ _____ or permanent, _____ damage to the brain.
9. Alcohol is involved in _____ percent of child abuse cases, _____ percent of all broken homes, and _____ of all homicides.
10. _____ _____ is the nation's most frequently committed violent crime.
11. Wine in ancient times was _____ than it is today.
12. It is best for a Christian to _____ completely from the consumption of alcohol.

Discussion
1. Why is drinking such a strong temptation for teenagers? What are some things you can do to resist this temptation?
2. Why would drinking in the first century *not* justify drinking in the twenty-first century?
3. What is the best thing to do when you find yourself around alcoholic beverages?
4. What could you say or do for a Christian who is struggling with drinking?

12
Stand Against Addiction

Most of us have a picture in our minds of what hell will be like. We imagine a place swarming with seditious foes of God, who stand squarely opposed to all that is good. However, this idea may need a little fine tuning. Hell will not only be populated by willing disciples of Satan. Its borders will also be stretched to include men and women who wanted to do good but failed. As the old adage goes, "The road to hell is paved with good intentions." Sadly, many people will never see the gates of heaven because they tried to fight an inner struggle against addiction, and they lost.

In Romans 7:24, Paul expressed the cry of the addicted: "Wretched man that I am!" These are the words of the smoker, the drug addict, and the alcoholic. They are uttered by desperate individuals hooked on pornography, gambling, and foul speech. Sometimes they are heard passing through the lips of those who are simply addicted to work or recreation. Wherever they are heard, they represent a pitiful state of being.

This lesson will address the need for young people to stand against harmful addictions. The Bible is a book of hope--even in the case of the addict. Its message reveals how we may be set free from the things that enslave us.

Understanding Addiction

Usually the word "addiction" denotes a harmful

behavior over which a person has lost control. Even after repeated attempts to stop, one may not be able to overcome his particular habit. The apostle Paul described this mindset when he said, "For although they knew God, they did not honor him as God or give thanks to him, but they became futile in their thinking, and their foolish hearts were darkened" (Romans 1:21). When one is addicted to some substance or behavior, he does not behave sensibly. He is a slave with "futile" thought processes and a "foolish," "darkened" heart.

The Bible uses interesting language to describe addiction. Often it is said that people oppressed by their own bad habits are "full of" sin, as if they were saturated with evil. For instance, Jesus said the Pharisees were "full of greed and self-indulgence" (Matthew 23:25). Also, some have mouths "full of curses and bitterness" (Romans 3:14). Peter condemned false teachers who had "eyes full of adultery, insatiable for sin" (2 Peter 2:14). Of the Gentiles, Paul wrote, "They were filled with all manner of unrighteousness, evil, covetousness, malice. They are full of envy, murder, strife, deceit, maliciousness…" (Romans 1:29).

Without question, addictions are extremely dangerous. Consider some of their harmful characteristics:
- They take otherwise wholesome human urges and abuse them, making them sinful.
- They expend enormous amounts of time that could be spent on worthy endeavors.
- Rarely do bad habits lead to progress or productivity of any kind.
- Addictions "lock" an individual into a sinful holding pattern.
- As one continues to remain in the grip of a harmful addiction, he builds a "tolerance" to whatever is consuming him—be it drugs, sex, or gambling—and so he must feed his urges more to achieve the same

- level of gratification.
- Addictions never bring satisfaction; they always leave their victim wanting more.
- If a person is unable to break his sinful habit before his death, he will have to stand condemned before God.

Certain substances such as nicotine (contained in tobacco), cocaine, and heroin are physically addictive. This means that the body itself is addicted to the substance and will suffer withdrawal symptoms when deprived of it. Because certain substances are physically addictive, some professionals prefer to call this problem a "disease." It is understandable that addictions can get out of control, and sometimes medical attention is required, but I would hesitate to designate substance abuse in this way. If this is a disease, it is a strange one! It is the only disease contracted by choice or regulated by law. Also, it is the only disease that has to be purchased with money and that has no germ or virus. Also, if substance abuse is a disease, it is the only disease that will condemn you to hell!

It is true that physical addictions are quite oppressive. However, they can be overcome. The church at Corinth had dealt with awful sins, several of which would be classified as addictive today:

> Do you not know that the unrighteous will not inherit the kingdom of God? Do not be deceived: neither the sexually immoral, nor idolaters, nor adulterers, nor men who practice homosexuality, nor thieves, nor the greedy, nor drunkards, nor revilers, nor swindlers will inherit the kingdom of God" (1 Corinthians 6:9-10).

Thankfully, Paul could speak of them in the past tense: "And such were some of you. But you were washed, you were sanctified, you were justified in the name of the Lord Jesus Christ and by the Spirit of our God" (1 Corinthians 6:11). With help from God, they were able to overcome the sin that ensnared them!

Breaking Bad Habits

How can I make a firm stand against harmful addictions? Here are a few suggestions revealed from God's word.

Take preventive measures.

The best time to overcome addiction is *before* you take the first smoke, drink the first drink, or give in to sinful lust. When it comes to avoiding bad habits, prevention is the best medicine. Take the advice of an old country doctor who was approached by a patient complaining that he broke his arm in two places. He said, "Don't go in them two places." Maybe his medical advice was confused, but his words are sound advice to young people facing temptation. Romans 13:14 says, "But put on the Lord Jesus Christ, and make no provision for the flesh, to gratify its desires" (cf. Proverbs 4:14-15).

Of course, not everybody can follow this suggestion. Some are already in the throes of addiction and need advice on how to escape. If you can no longer take preventive measures, there is still hope for you...

Seek professional help.

As we have already said, many substances are physically addictive. This may make it necessary to seek professional care. When the body develops a dependence, medical or psychological treatment may be required. There are plenty of places to which one may go: rehabilitation clinics, doctors, counselors, therapists, etc. Sure, it may be embarrassing to bring a problem with substance abuse into the open, but the pain of disclosing an awful secret is worth the end result.

Professional care can be very helpful in overcoming addictions, but one must not stop there. Life is incomplete without God. Only He can fill the void left by an enslavement to sin.

Follow a new law.

The closest we get to a biblical description of the inner struggle of an addict is found in Romans chapter 7. According to what we read in verses 22-24, this "slavery" occurs when two different laws fight for control of the heart in the inward man.

> For I delight in the law of God, in my inner being, but I see in my members another law waging war against the law of my mind and making me captive to the law of sin that dwells in my members. Wretched man that I am! Who will deliver me from this body of death?

The law of God, of course, is what is good for man. It will lead him to contentment and joy. However, when a person is caught in a sinful addiction, "another law," "the law of sin," gets the upper hand. This law appeals to the flesh and originates from the lies of Satan himself (John 8:44).

How can a person be released from the "law of sin?" This question is answered in the next chapter: "There is therefore now no condemnation for those who are in Christ Jesus. For the law of the Spirit of life has set you free in Christ Jesus from the law of sin and death" (Romans 8:1-2). To overcome addiction, follow a new law: "the law of the Spirit of life." This law has graciously been revealed to us in the New Testament (2 Timothy 3:16-17; 2 Peter 1:20-21).

Find productive work to do.

Once you are released from the oppression of addiction, your work is not done. There is an old saying, "Idleness is the devil's workshop." Those words are particularly true in relation to overcoming bad habits. In order to beat addiction and avoid relapse, you must find something productive to do.

Addictions cannot be overcome by focusing only on avoiding sinful habits. This will just cause you to concentrate on the problem more. A more balanced approach is needed. Consider both sides of the formula revealed in Romans 6:12-13:

> Let not sin therefore reign in your mortal bodies, to make you obey their passions. Do not present your members to sin as instruments for unrighteousness, but present yourselves to God as those who have been brought from death to life, and your members to God as instruments for righteousness.

In the first place, Paul admonishes his readers never to yield their members as "instruments for unrighteousness," but that is only half of the battle. After that is done, one must yield himself unto God as an "instrument for righteousness." After the addiction is overcome, it must be replaced with something better—something useful, something wholesome.

Many times, a person will fall into a sinful habit because he seeks an escape from his problems. Of course, things like drug abuse, alcoholism, smoking, gambling, and pornography provide no such escape; they only compound the problem. If someone is able to overcome an addiction, this does not guarantee a life free of challenges or troubles. Are there wholesome, useful activities to which we may turn when we need a temporary escape from our problems?

Look to Jesus for examples of healthy forms of escape. While on earth, He was constantly handling the pressures of His ministry in healthy, constructive ways.

When Jesus needed a break from his problems, He *related*. Often He would spend time with close friends. Mark 3:14 reads, "And he appointed twelve (whom he also named apostles) so that they might be with him and he might send them out to preach." We think of the apostles as mere instruments of Christ, hand-picked to do His bidding. However, Mark tells us Christ also chose them "that they might be with him." He needed co-workers, but He also needed friends. As the Lord worked in the city of Jerusalem, one would find Him withdrawing at night to a little village named Bethany (Mark 11:11-12). Why go to the trouble of leaving town in the evenings and returning the next day? John gives us the explanation, "Now a certain man was ill, Lazarus of Bethany, the village of Mary and her sister Martha...Now Jesus loved Martha and her sister and Lazarus" (John 11:1, 5). Bethany was important to Jesus because that is where His friends lived.

When he wanted an escape, Jesus also *retreated*. Matthew 14 describes a stressful day in the life of Christ. It begins with news of the death of John the Baptist, Jesus' cousin and co-worker. Wanting some time to deal with this, Jesus tried to withdraw from the people in a boat, but the crowds learned of His plans and found Him. Although He was emotionally strained, He had compassion on the multitude and healed their sick. He also fed them, 5,000 men besides women and children, with only five loaves and two fish. Can you imagine how exhausted He was? He had suffered sorrow over the news of John, the strain of working with people, and the fatigue that comes with a long, rigorous day. A day like this might cause some to escape to alcohol or some behavior designed to satisfy sinful lust. But Jesus retreated:

> Immediately he made the disciples get into the boat and go before him to the other side, while he dismissed the crowds. And after he had dismissed the crowds, he went up on the mountain by himself to pray. When evening came, he was there alone (Matthew 14:22-23).

Notice that it got to the point that Jesus had to seize control. He "made" (literally, "forced") the disciples to get into a boat and sail ahead of Him on the Sea of Galilee. He "dismissed" the crowds. Things were not going to slow down unless He took charge. But He did not resort to anger; He did not grow impatient. He just let the people know that it was time for Him to be alone. He retreated, and by evening He was alone.

Your personal retreat may not be the solitude of a mountain. It may be fishing, golf, or music. It may involve physical exercise or maybe a period of meditation. The point is that there are many wholesome, constructive activities that can be used as forms of escape from the pressures of the world.

The Lord also *reflected*. This was really the reason why He retreated so often to the mountains. There He could contemplate His mission and how He could overcome the forces seeking to destroy Him. This period of reflection always involved prayer (Luke 5:16; 6:12; et al.). Even Jesus knew that, when He wanted to avoid anxiety, He could communicate with the Father. Accordingly, Paul instructs us,

> Do not be anxious about anything, but in everything by prayer and supplication with thanksgiving let your requests be made known to God. And the peace of God, which surpasses all understanding, will guard your hearts and your minds in Christ Jesus (Philippians 4:6-7).

Nobody wants to be a slave to sin. Follow these four suggestions, and you can be set free from the bondage of sinful habits.

In actuality, we are all slaves. Either we are slaves of sin, or we are slaves of righteousness (Romans 6:15-18). Unfortunately, too many people are slaves of sin and find themselves heading down a deadly path. If you are one of these people, there is good news for you: Maybe we are all slaves, but we don't have to keep the same master! Take a stand against harmful addictions, and make Jesus the master of your life.

Exercises

Fill In The Blanks
1. Paul expressed the cry of the addicted when he said, "_____ man that I am!"
2. The word "addicted" denotes a harmful behavior over which a person has lost _____.
3. The Bible often describes someone addicted to sinful behavior as being _____ _____ sin.
4. Addictions take otherwise wholesome human _____ and abuse them.
5. As one continues to remain in the grip of an addiction, he builds a _____ to whatever is consuming him.
6. Some substances are _____ addictive.
7. The best time to overcome addiction is _____ you take the first smoke, drink the first drink, or give in to sinful lust.
8. Those who are physically addicted may need to seek _____ help.
9. To overcome addiction, one must follow the _____ of the _____ of life.
10. "Idleness is the _____ workshop."
11. In order to beat addiction and avoid relapse, you must find something _____ to do.
12. Jesus gives us a number of examples of healthy forms of _____.

Discussion
1. Can you think of some addictions that were not addressed in this lesson? Will the things we discussed help overcome these problems as well?
2. What are some constructive forms of escape that you use to help you avoid sin? Do you have any hobbies or places to which you go for rest?
3. What can you do to help a friend who is suffering from a harmful addiction?

13

Stand Against Peer Pressure

As I was preparing to write this book, I conducted an informal survey among young people. I asked, "Why is it difficult to take a stand?" As I expected, there was a variety of answers. One responded that "horrible social anxiety" made it hard to take a stand. Another said, "I guess the thing that makes it most difficult is that I really don't want to offend my friends...I guess I'm afraid of someone being mad at me." Someone else wrote, "People will always make fun of you...sometimes you have to feel alone." The answers were different, and yet they all seemed to have something in common. One particular theme surfaced in every answer I received: *peer pressure*.

Peer pressure challenges all of us, but young people are especially touched by its power to influence in one direction or another. In his book *The Tale of the Tardy Oxcart*, Charles Swindoll illustrates this fact by telling of an interesting experiment conducted with teenagers. Some psychologists brought groups of ten young people into a room for a test. Each group of ten was instructed to raise their hands when the teacher pointed to the longest line on a chart. What one person in the group did not know was that nine of the others in the room had been instructed ahead of time to vote for the second-longest line. Almost without exception, when the nine voted for the wrong line, the tenth teenager (the one who had been left in the dark) would glance around, frown in confusion, and finally slip his hand up with the group. Amazingly, a young person caved to peer pressure in seventy-five percent of the cases, even when it was obvious he was making the wrong choice.[1] There should be no doubt that the influence of one's friends is powerful—even when it heads in the wrong direction!

The Power of Peer Pressure

Why is it so hard to stand against peer pressure? When you study the matter closely, it becomes apparent that there are three intense forces that feed its power.

The Force of Influence

Long ago, astrologers believed celestial fluids flowed from the stars and affected the characters and actions of people. This "in flow" was thought to be responsible, at least in part, for one's personality, his successes and failures, and even his fate in life. As science progressed, the affects of "in flow" continued to be watched, but ideas concerning the stars as its source were dropped. Soon "in flow" came to be known as "influence," and it became clear that the character and actions of people are not affected by the stars, but by the character and actions of other people.[16]

The force of influence is affirmed many times in the Bible. Solomon wrote, "Whoever walks with the wise becomes wise, but the companion of fools will suffer harm" (Proverbs 13:20). He should have listened to his own advice, for later he let 700 wives and 300 concubines turn his heart from following the Lord (1 Kings 11:3-4). Paul said, "Do not be deceived: Bad company ruins good morals" (1 Corinthians 15:33). Three times, the Bible compares evil influences with "leaven" (Luke 12:1; 1 Corinthians 5:6-8; Galatians 5:7-9). Leaven, or yeast, is used in baking to make dough rise. The substance is a fitting illustration of the power of influence because only a small amount is needed to affect the whole lump of dough.

Some of the greatest downfalls in history were due to the force of influence. Eve was manipulated by the serpent, and Adam was manipulated by his wife. So the perfection of man came down in one felled swoop due to the influence of the devil! Another example of the power of influence for evil is Jezebel. Concerning the wickedness of the kings of Israel, we are told, "There was none who sold himself to do what was evil in the sight of the Lord like Ahab." But why had he stooped so low? "Jezebel his wife incited [him]" (1 Kings 21:25).

However, it is also true that some of the greatest triumphs in history were due to good influences. Timothy was great because he had been influenced by his grandmother Lois and his mother Eunice (2 Timothy 1:5). Also, the people of Israel repented when they saw Ezra the scribe weep over sin (Ezra 10:1). Influence can be a force for evil or good. Its direction depends on those who wield it.

Peer pressure can be tough because it involves influence. This is important to understand, especially when you are tempted to hang around with the wrong crowd. Some young people object to warnings about peer pressure, saying, "They won't drag me down. I'm going to influence them for good!" These are noble but foolish words. They ignore the forceful influence behind peer pressure. Abraham Lincoln once said, "When you have got an elephant by the hind leg, and he is trying to run away, it's best to let him run." Too many teenagers lose their souls because they don't understand the power of influence and won't let go of an "elephant's hind leg."

The Force of Friendship

When God created man, He said, "It is not good that

the man should be alone..." (Genesis 2:18). From that point forward, companionship has become an intricate part of human life.

Having understood the power of influence, we recognize that nobody has more influence over us than our friends. True friends love us at all times (Proverbs 17:17), and friendships make life worthwhile. As Robert Louis Stevenson said, "So long as we are loved by others, I would almost say that we are indispensable; and no man is useless while he has a friend."

But be careful. Looks can be deceiving. A person who appears to be a friend is not always a *true* friend. David often lamented the treatment he received at the hands of his so-called "friends" (Psalm 35:11-16; 41:9; 55:12-14). Also, Solomon warns us, saying, "A man of many companions may come to ruin..." (Proverbs 18:24). We must be cautious of "friends" who come easily and in great numbers. Sadly, in some cases it is better to be alone than to have a particular person as a friend. Jesus is not the only person who has been betrayed by a friend (Matthew 26:48-49).

Peer pressure can be very difficult to withstand, especially when it comes from friends. Therefore, we ought to take great care in choosing companions. Sometimes your best friend can also be your worst enemy.

The Force of Fear

Peer pressure also includes a measure of fear. All kinds of scary thoughts pop into our heads when we are faced with it: "What if they make fun of me? What if they think I'm a nerd? Will anybody want to be with me if I stand up for what is right? What if they get angry? Will they hurt me? Will I be alone?"

These fears are natural. Everybody from time to

time makes decisions that cause them to clash against the times. As someone has said, "Only dead fish swim with the current all the time." However, if you are a Christian, it may seem that your life is clashing more often than not. Jesus explained why when He said, "If you were of the world, the world would love you as its own; but because you are not of the world, but I chose you out of the world, therefore the world hates you" (John 15:19). Because Christians are "not of the world," the world is not going to like them very much.

Anyone who wants to stand against the power of peer pressure has got to come to grips with fear. A strategy has to be developed to face courageously opposition and persecution. In a word, that strategy is faith. Believe that God will give you the strength to endure (Philippians 4:13). Believe that with Him all things are possible (Matthew 19:26). Believe that, "If God is for us, who can be against us?" (Romans 8:31). Believe that your reward is great in heaven (Matthew 5:10-12; John 14:1-3). Jesus once asked His disciples, "Why are you afraid, O you of little faith?" (Matthew 8:26). He asks us the same question every time we let the world intimidate us.

Behind peer pressure are the forces of influence, friendship, and fear. As we acknowledge its power, we can learn how to deal with it.

A Case Study in Handling Peer Pressure: Peter and Paul

Peter and Paul were both apostles. They both loved Christ and His cause. Both of them fought hard for the things they believed in. Beyond this, they were two very different men.

Peter was emotional. He was the one who drew his sword and cut off Malchus' ear. He preferred jumping out of a boat and swimming to Christ rather than waiting to float to shore (John 21:7-8).

Paul on the other hand was intellectual. He is known for his philosophical approach to Christianity. He did not act on instinct, but upon his knowledge of Jesus Christ (Philippians 3:8; 2 Timothy 1:12). Even when he was way off base, persecuting Christians as Saul of Tarsus, he lived his life "in all good conscience" (Acts 23:1).

These differences affected the way these two apostles dealt with peer pressure. Through a letter of Paul's, we can observe how that, when faced with negative influences, one stood firm while the other caved.

> But when Cephas [Peter] came to Antioch, I opposed him to his face, because he stood condemned. For before certain men came from James, he was eating with the Gentiles, but when they came he drew back and separated himself, fearing the circumcision party. And the rest of the Jews acted hypocritically along with him, so that even Barnabas was led astray by their hypocrisy. But when I saw that their conduct was not in step with the truth of the gospel, I said to Cephas before them all, "If you, though a Jew, live like a Gentile and not like a Jew, how can you force the Gentiles to live like Jews?" (Galatians 2:11-14).

What did Peter do?

Peter had learned first hand that the gospel was for all nations, Jews and Gentiles (Acts 10:34-35). In fact, Paul said that he was eating with the Gentiles. But that all changed upon the arrival of a group Paul referred to as the "circumcision party." These men carried the full force of peer pressure. They were influential, they were friends, and Peter was afraid of them. These men purported to be "from James." James was a powerful leader in the church at Jerusalem, the most influential congregation in the church. He was somebody Peter wanted to impress. If these men were friends of James, then in Peter's mind they were friends of his. In Paul's words, these were false teachers who wanted to "force the Gentiles to live like Jews." Later James would tell Peter, Paul, and several others that, while these men had come from him, he had not agreed with their position (Acts 15:24). But for the moment, Peter thought his reputation was at stake, and he did not want to lose the favor of his friends back in Jerusalem.

So when he was faced with peer pressure, he "drew back and separated himself" from the Gentiles. This action wasn't based on any firm conviction or knowledge of the scriptures, for he acted "hypocritically." The primary motivation was fear of the circumcision party. The others caved with him. Even Barnabas was led astray.

What did Paul do?

It didn't matter to Paul that these men claimed to come from James. They could have come from Caesar—he wasn't going to pervert the truth. When he saw that Peter and the others were not "in step with the truth," he boldly opposed them. We are grateful. If he had not, a rift might have formed that would have divided the church between Jews and Gentiles to this day!

Which apostle best represents you? Are you a Peter, or are you a Paul? When it comes to your moral stance, are you guided by the truth or craven fear?

Peer pressure is a tough challenge for us all. But we must put our faith in God. And don't worry. You are not alone. Like Elijah, you have "seven thousand" companions who have also stood firm against the weight of the world (1 Kings 19:18).

Exercises

Fill In The Blanks
1. Long ago, _____ believed celestial fluids from the stars affected the _____ and _____ of people.
2. Solomon had _____ wives and _____ concubines.
3. "A little _____ leavens the whole lump" (1 Corinthians 5:6; Galatians 5:9).
4. Ahab was influenced by his wife _____.
5. "It is not good that the man should be _____" (Genesis 2:18).
6. A person who appears to be a friend is not always a _____ friend.
7. "A man of many companions may come to _____" (Proverbs 18:24).
8. The world _____ Christians (John 15:19).
9. With _____ all things are possible.
10. Peter was _____.
11. Paul was _____.
12. Peter and Paul's disagreement came up when they were visited by the _____ party.

Discussion
1. What are some things you are tempted to do because of peer pressure?
2. Who exerts a positive influence over you? Who usually exerts a negative influence over you? What kind of influence do you exert over your friends?
3. What are some fears that go along with peer pressure?
4. Is your personality more like Peter's or Paul's? Does this affect how you handle peer pressure?

Endnotes

[1] Ralph Gilmore, "Postmodernism: Change in World View/Change in Truth View," *Freed-Hardeman University 1998 Lectures*, Ed., David Lipe (Henderson: FHU, 1998), p. 137.

[2] John Leo, "A No-Fault Holocaust," *U.S. News and World Report* (July 21, 1997), p. 14.

[3] Clint Bonner, *A Hymn Is Born* (Nashville: Broadman Press, 1959), pp. 84-85.

[4] *Christianity Today* (October 26, 1992), p. 30.

[5] Michael W. Holmes, Ed., *The Apostolic Fathers* (Grand Rapids: Baker Book House, 1992), pp. 233-41.

[6] Thomas B. Warren, *The Warren-Flew Debate* (Jonesboro: National Christian Press, 1977), pp. 37-42.

[7] C.S. Lewis, *Mere Christianity* (New York: Macmillan, 1943), p. 31.

[8] Bert Thompson, *Rock Solid Faith: How to Build It* (Montgomery: Apologetics Press, 2000), p. 216.

[9] John R.W. Stott, *The Message of Galatians* (Downers Grove: Inter-Varsity Press, 1968), p. 156.

[10] Helen and Martin Weiss, "Building Confidence and Self-Esteem," *Summit Daily News* (May 30, 2003).

[11] Tom Scarritt, "To Raise Self-Esteem, Earn It," *The Birmingham News* (April 27, 2003).

[12] Walter Berry, "Giant Bird's Penchant For People Results in Return to Captivity," *The Birmingham News* (April 25, 1999), p. 8a.

[13] R.C.H. Lenski, *The Interpretation of St. Matthew's Gospel* (Hendrickson Publishers, 2001), p. 300.

[14] W.E. Vine, *Vine's Expository Dictionary of New Testament Words* (McLean: Macdonald Publishing Co.), p. 761.

[15] Statistics taken from Mike Benson, "Support The Sponsor," *Words of Truth* (June 2003), p. 6, and www.madd.org.

[16] *Webster's New World Collegiate Dictionary*.

Also available through
Riddle Creek Publishing

<u>To the Overcomers</u> by Andy Kizer
<u>Wisdom's Call</u> by Drew Kizer
<u>The Cast of the Cross</u> by Drew Kizer
<u>Be Wise God's Way</u> by Adam Faughn
<u>From Slaves to Conquerors</u> by Barton Kizer
<u>Marriage and the Christian Home</u> by Dr. Ted Burleson
<u>Who Knew?</u>
Records of Divine Providence by Andy Kizer
<u>From Conquerors to Kings</u> by Drew Kizer
<u>The 15 Periods of Bible History *Revised*</u> by Andy Kizer

Riddle Creek Pocket Guides
Five Class Sessions

"Psalms and the Issues"
"Instructions for Successful Living"
"Families with a Focus"

A useful tool for camp counselors, youth ministers, retreat leaders, Bible class teachers and more